CRAZY
Like
FOXES

By
Bob Williamson and Jamie Vrinios

CRAZY *Like* FOXES

by
Bob Williamson and Jamie Vrinios

For information write Williamson Publishing, 416 N. Adams St., Tallahassee, Florida 32301

Book Design: CuneoCreative.com

ISBN 978-0-692-82120-6

First Edition

*This book is dedicated
to those courageous souls
who will read it,
follow their dreams,
and soar like eagles.*

CRAZY *Like* FOXES

Table of Contents

INTRODUCTION

What Does It Take to Succeed?

Bob Williamson

This question has been asked by millions of people since the dawn of time, and hordes of successful people all over the world have been more than willing to share their version of how they or others did it via books, seminars, and coaching events galore.

So I was initially reluctant to write yet another book on this subject, primarily because it seemed so unnecessary. I changed my mind after meeting and getting to know Jamie Vrinios. One of my friends told me she was a fascinating speaker with an inspirational and riveting story, and recommended I ask Jamie to appear at our church, which I did.

And she didn't disappoint. After hearing her motivational story, I was intrigued by how she (like me) had overcome the enormous obstacles she faced and become wildly successful.

Some months later Jamie invited me to speak at one of her many business conferences. I gave an account of my life and how I was able to climb out of the pit and succeed. Afterward, she shared her strikingly similar story, and then we appeared together on stage to answer questions. The combination of two dramatically different people, who both overcame a lack of education, money and support from family or friends to become tremendously successful, profoundly struck a chord with the audience.

A few days later, Jamie called to tell me she'd had many requests from people who would like to hear more from us. She wondered out loud if we could speak together at additional events, and maybe even write a book.

Hmmm.

Our differences are obvious. I'm a man, and she is a woman. She is young, fiery, and trendy. I'm older, more measured and reserved. But we are similar in that we both started at rock bottom and fought our way up; we both have grit and dogged tenacity; and we both are totally devoted to keep fighting as long as we can take a breath. Ours are genuine rags-to-riches stories.

Like I said, I'm aware that there are many such stories, but what makes ours unique is that in spite of tough circumstances early in life and striking differences, we succeeded using very similar methodology. In fact, our stories clearly demonstrate that even people with vastly different backgrounds can follow the same path to success.

As Jamie and I discussed it more, we became convinced that because we could conquer the obstacles of life and reach the pinnacle of success, then *anyone* can. So we set out on the adventure of documenting in our own words exactly how each of us did it. We hope this book leads you to your dreams.

Nonetheless, if you're looking for a book that explains the finer points of success as taught at Yale, Harvard, or the Wharton School of Business, then you have chosen the wrong book. Our stories are not technical textbook treatises or even theories offered by college professors, some of whom have never built anything themselves. Rather, our accounts track our personal journeys from the mean streets to easy street. We believe that the lessons we learned will help you follow the same path if you adhere to them.

To write this book, we started by agreeing on the general topics most instrumental to our success. Then we wrote about them independently, using our individual life experiences to illustrate our approaches. As you'll see, it's a fascinating and educational collaboration.

As far as I can tell, no one has ever written a book like this. Even if someone has, I am dead certain that this one will help anyone who reads it reach his or her seemingly unreachable goals.

And finally, you may be wondering why we titled it *Crazy Like Foxes*. We almost called it *Against All Odds* or *How We Did It*, but we picked this name because we had both been called "crazy" numerous times by negative people who told us we were doomed to fail.

Actually, in retrospect, they were right. We were crazy.

Crazy Like Foxes!

BOB WILLIAMSON AND JAMIE VRINIOS

INTRODUCTION

What Does It Take to Succeed?

Jamie Vrinios

Let me begin by saying it was absolutely a LONG SHOT that two people like Bob and I came together to UNLEASH this message of RAW, REAL TRUTH to the world. I can tell you that NEVER in a MILLION YEARS would I have thought TWO very separate and far different WORLDS could collide. It confirms for me that God has a GREAT sense of humor. Many people believe that if the path to a dream isn't smooth and easy then it isn't meant to be, or even worth the effort. I believe the opposite. My life experiences and successes have taught me that the path of least resistance leads only to average.

This book is not for the faint of heart; it is for those who desire to unleash their greatest potential with reckless abandon. The mind-set you create from the beginning determines the path you choose, and your destination arrival time is contingent upon how you respond to LIFE. We all face obstacles, and our choice is to either pursue your dream or settle for merely existing day to day. It is entirely up to you. If I based my life on a negative point of view I would have given up at the beginning.

Truth: I was BRAVE enough to BEGIN again and again no matter what was required of me.

What is your mind-set at this moment? Are you

determined to turn the pages of this book even if the pages pierce your soul?

I encourage you to read with an OPEN mind and HEART and to be BRAVE enough to make the changes necessary to achieve the OUTRAGEOUS. Keep in mind that all BRAVE BEGINNINGS require TRANSFORMATION, and the journey is not about how fast we reach our destination but rather who we become in the process. We can't smother our dreams with fear and doubt and a book full of rules. Instead we must give them room to breathe. I encourage you to throw away any previous rules that have hindered you, press the reset button, and start over.

Imagine all the mistakes you've made in your life have been thrown into the ocean with a big sign that says No Fishing Allowed. Our dreams can never be full of LIFE unless we say good-bye to the demons of our past and break the chains that hold us back. I can promise you this: When you commit to seeing your dreams manifest themselves as reality, there will be naysayers who'll consistently try to "fish" into the past in order to hold you back from tomorrow. So before we move forward, promise yourself that you will have a funeral today with the past and BEGIN ANEW.

Truth: By the time you finish this book, I know you will see why God brought Bob's story and my story together.

In my experience, when we meet obstacles we must be more determined to press on, because that is where growth BEGINS. Unfortunately, there will be FEW who dare to take the LONG SHOTS in life, and to the FEW who do, I applaud you.

It is a FACT that the FEW can impact the masses, if they are brave enough to LEAD. Even if you don't make it past the first few pages, I believe one day you will pick this book up again and DARE to embrace your crazy, awe-inspiring dream. This book can be pivotal in encouraging you along the way and helping you create an UNSHAKEABLE MIND-SET, which is necessary to achieve what the naysayers of the world may say is impossible.

BOB WILLIAMSON AND JAMIE VRINIOS

CHAPTER 1

Long Shots

Bob Williamson

Many people have low self-esteem. I had it and for good reason. I'd been told I was stupid, lazy, incompetent, and worthless all of my early life. It had a devastating effect because I believed all of it.

This chapter deals with self-esteem. I believe the Bible when it states that God created each of us to fulfill a specific purpose. He fearfully and wonderfully shaped us in the womb and equipped us with every attribute necessary to accomplish His purpose, and it's our job to realize it and claim it. I did, and so can you.

This chapter is the longest one in the book. That's how important we think this subject is! It details how Jamie and I, who were considered long shots at succeeding at anything, overcame our low self-esteem and profited at many things.

I've lived the kind of life most people only dream about —many of those dreams began as chilling nightmares, but I've had more than my fair share of years that were ridiculously luxuriant and even glorious. I've about seen and done it all. I've experienced the highest of highs and the lowest of lows. Each towering pinnacle was reached from a deep gorge, and the climbs have always been filled with made-for-Hollywood drama.

Check out my résumé. I've been a homeless drifter who hitchhiked and hopped freight trains all over North

America, an armed robber, a forger, an inmate (at one of the most violent prisons in the United States), a diagnosed sociopath who was kicked out of the military, a sadistic street fighter, an alcoholic, an intravenous methamphetamine/heroin addict, a drug dealer, a divorcé, a multiple near-death survivor, a loner, an atheist, an agnostic, and even a warlock. Then I became a born-again evangelical Christian, a family man, a company man, a software pioneer, a serial entrepreneur, an inventor, a white-collar fraud victim, a publishing impresario, an artist, a playboy, a husband, father, and grandfather, an author, a resort-and-spa developer and owner, a worldwide networker, a church and global ministry founder, a philanthropist, a lifesaver, a consultant, an oracle, and a multimillionaire.

Hmmm. I wonder what you're thinking right now.

Lol! I've done thousands of television and radio appearances and had articles written about me by some of the most vaunted outlets, including *Reader's Digest, Forbes, Huffington Post, INC. magazine, Business Week,* AOL, MSNBC, and CNN. Invariably when their fact-checkers hear my story, they seem to rub their hands eagerly in anticipation of debunking me as a myth. But after their exhaustive and collective careful research, they have come away shaking their heads and wondering how one person could have done so much (and actually lived through it).

Most people (including me) can hardly believe it, but I assure you it's true. Oddly, I view myself as just an everyday guy trying to build a happy, stable, sober life—but it's a life in which there has rarely been a dull moment.

I recently read the best-selling biography *Unbroken*, by Laura Hillenbrand, and watched its adaptation to the big screen with much admiration and appreciation for its subject, Louis Zamperini. His courageous journey included transitioning from juvenile delinquency to Olympian, joining the U.S. Army Air Forces during World War II, and surviving a plane crash in the Pacific Ocean. Stranded on a raft with two other crewmen, he endured thirst, hunger, enemy aircraft fire, sharks, storms, and relentless heat. One man died on day 33, but Zamperini prevailed.

He prayed for himself and his surviving crewmate, vowing that if God saved them, he would serve heaven forever. On the 47th day in a raft, his prayer was answered (at least in part) when a Japanese naval ship picked them up. They were sent to a prisoner of war camp, where a depraved Japanese commander beat and tortured them. Driven to the limits of endurance, Zamperini overcame the brutality and suffering through faith and hope, along with a stubborn rebellious attitude and sheer will power. He emerged "unbroken."

While reading about Zamperini's struggles, I thought of my own life journey and how I, too, had faced seemingly insurmountable obstacles. I noted the similarities between Zamperini's character and my own. We both possessed tough, stubborn, rebellious attitudes, refusing to quit and fighting defiantly and furiously, determined to never let anyone or anything deter us.

As I look back on my many years of disappointment, disillusionment, setback, and tragedy and reflect on how often I reacted violently and self-destructively in those situations, I can't believe I'm not now in prison, an insane asylum, or dead. Like Zamperini, I am a survivor.

But that is where our similarities end. I made it only because I became completely *broken* and finally surrendered.

My early home life was dysfunctional. My mother was an atheist, and my father was also far from religion, although that dramatically changed for them later in life. We didn't go to church, and I was glad—I wanted no part of it. I thought church people were weak hypocrites.

My father did not like me AT ALL, but he revered my brother and worshipped my mother. Why he disliked me I'll never know. He died at 92 without telling me. I always suspected he thought I was the result of my mother having an affair, but I exhibited too many Williamson characteristics to believe that. His disdain for me started early enough in my life (as far back as I can remember) for it to have been caused by something I did to him. I still wonder about it.

My mother did not dislike me, but like my father she was enamored with my brother. He was their golden boy who could do no wrong, and I was the "bad seed" who could do nothing right. Most of the time they ignored me, which was preferable to being noticed and subjected to severe beatings by my enraged father. At the end of each day, I suffered from a broken heart and felt completely alone.

My father was in the military for most of the time I lived at home, and military life meant we moved frequently. I attended 19 schools in about as many states and two different countries. I went to three high schools. Forming lasting friendships or finding a coach or teacher mentor was not possible. As soon as I was nearly acclimated to new surroundings, we moved somewhere else far away.

The combination of verbal and mental abuse, sibling rivalry, absence of love, and instability had a devastating effect on me. Eventually, I became a stone-cold loner filled with bitterness, hatred, and rage. Such antisocial behavior had me in and out of jails (most times for fighting). I fought almost every day and was known for being sadistically cruel. And my mean streak grew meaner with each passing year. I began with fists, graduated to brass knuckles, then a baseball bat, and finally to a chrome-plated .357 Magnum revolver and a sawed-off shotgun.

That was my progression (or better, regression).

I tried a number of things to relieve my misery. I began by drinking (I was an alcoholic by age 13). Then I started using illegal drugs, including pot, psychedelics such as LSD, opiates, and methamphetamine (my favorite). I was an animal when it came to taking drugs. I took huge amounts and overdosed twice, nearly dying. One time my liver stopped functioning for about a week.

I lived in the Haight-Ashbury district of San Francisco during the birth of the illegal-drug and free-love revolution. When alcohol and drugs didn't relieve my misery, I resorted to uninhibited sex with numerous women. But that didn't drown my pain either. These encounters were just temporary highs that left me lower than before.

When all these excesses failed to fill what was missing in my life, I turned to attaining and exercising power over others—I began committing dangerous violent crimes such as robbing people at gunpoint. In this same vein, I learned witchcraft and black magic to further dominate and manifest my power over others. It worked for a while, my mood lifted with each rush of adrenaline, but it too faded, leaving me feeling foul and dreadful. None of it ever helped, and in fact, it all made matters worse.

I had an opportunity to "go normal" when I married at 19. But true to form, in just 11 months the relationship ended in a nasty divorce that swept away my first-born son, Jim, in its devastating wake.

Shortly afterward I was drafted and entered the military. To say I disliked the military is an understatement. The Vietnam War was raging, and it seemed ridiculous to me that our country interfered with those people. They'd been fighting civil wars for thousands of years, and they'd likely continue long after we were gone. I wasn't protecting our homeland from an imminent threat, and I saw no reason to travel halfway around the world to die in a rice paddy in some tiny country with which I had no quarrel. But I didn't really have a choice. And I thought maybe, just maybe, the military would straighten me out.

It didn't.

Six months later I was in a military prison in Buffalo, New York, awaiting court martial for some serious crimes. As part of my legal proceedings, four psychiatrists examined my thick file and questioned me for about four hours before sending me back to my cell. The next day the head "shrink" summoned me back and matter-of-factly told me I had been diagnosed as a sociopath. He asked if I knew what that meant, and I told him I did not.

He said, "It means you don't have a conscience, you feel

no remorse for anything you do, and you have no emotions or feelings for anyone aside from yourself." "Bob, you're incapable of love and, if I had to guess, *I'd say you're well on your way to becoming a serial killer.*"

Shocked, I stammered, "Well, what do I do about it?"

He shook his head and sadly said, "There is nothing you can do, son. It's incurable. Therefore, I'm recommending that you be discharged from the military." And with a grim look on his face he shook his head and muttered, "Good luck."

In a few months I became a civilian again and returned to terrorizing the mean streets, this time in the Big Easy, New Orleans. I tried my utmost to live up to my sociopath diagnosis. In a very short period, I earned the reputation in the French Quarter of being a psychotic intravenous meth addict with a death wish. Everyone steered clear of me. I was always armed, crazy violent, callous, and fearless. I was dealing drugs, and woe to anyone foolish enough to rip me off.

It turns out the New Orleans Police Department's finest, thanks to its many snitches, were also well aware of me and were neither amused nor impressed. They wanted me off their streets. The problem was the police couldn't catch me committing a crime or convince anyone to snitch in court, so they planted drugs on me. I landed in violent Parrish Prison, and I fit right in. But after a few months, the case against me fell apart, and I was back on the streets. I didn't learn anything in prison except how to be more violent and a smarter criminal, so as soon as I was free I picked up where I'd left off with a vengeance.

The police were not happy about my return. Soon I was tipped off that the cops were sweeping the French Quarter looking for me, and this time I'd be taken off the streets "for good." My tipster knew what he was talking about—he was a police officer himself, albeit a corrupt "mobbed-up" one. We were partners in dealing pharmaceutical morphine to heroin addicts out of a mob-owned drugstore. He even gave me one of the mug shots the police were passing around. On the back it stated I was wanted on numerous felony charges and to consider me "armed and extremely dangerous."

I narrowly escaped capture by immediately fleeing the city. All I took was a pillowcase stuffed with a toothbrush and one change of clothes—all my possessions in the world. I hitchhiked to Atlanta even though I'd never been there and didn't know a single person. It just seemed like a good place to elude my pursuers and keep my head down.

As fate would have it, I arrived in Atlanta at the intersection of Fairlie and Luckie streets, near the Greyhound bus terminal.

Although it was a crummy section of town, filled with drug addicts, winos, and homeless, I was indeed "fairly lucky" to have ended up in Atlanta as my place of refuge, because Atlanta eventually proved to be very good for me.

Penniless, I immediately sold a pint of blood for $7. With that, I rented a room for $3 a night in a flophouse and bought a candy bar, Coke, and cigarettes. But I needed more cash. The next morning I got a workforce job chipping mortar off bricks with a hatchet so they could be reused. It paid $15 a day. After a couple of days of this backbreaking work, I had enough money to go to a bar, where I promptly got into a fight and nearly killed a guy by breaking a beer bottle over his head and then stabbing him in the face with the broken end. The police were called, and when the officers started roughing me up and preparing to cuff me, several witnesses (including the victim) came forward to vouch that I was defending a woman whose husband was beating her. I narrowly escaped being hauled in.

By now I'd tried everything I could imagine to find peace, but I was still in a constant state of paranoia, always fearing someone would shoot me in the back of the head, beat me up, or knife me. I endlessly expected the police to kick my door down and haul me off to prison again. I was homeless, my family wanted nothing to do with me, and I did not have one friend in the world. I couldn't find what I needed in a bottle, a needle, a bedroom, or by sticking a gun in someone's face and watching the victim shake like an aspen leaf.

As far as I could tell I'd run out of options and lost all hope. It felt like a big hole had been ripped open in my heart, and it could not be filled. I was utterly despondent. Ultimately, I concluded that death by suicide was preferable to my miserable life. My grandfather, two of my uncles, and my only sibling, my brother Jim all committed suicide. It was in my DNA, so I guess it was only natural that I too wanted to die. To prepare, I began accumulating enough money to buy the right kind of drug cocktail, (a hot shot of pure heroin and an entire bottle of Quaaludes to be downed with a bottle of wine). I could just go to sleep and never wake up.

But before I could get my hands on the drugs, I got drunk one night and drove a borrowed car head-on into another car in a devastating collision. My head went through the windshield. I knocked the driver-side door from its hinges with my left shoulder. I broke the steering wheel off with my sternum. I was conscious for a moment after the crash and saw blood spurting all over the windshield that was located about 12 inches from my face. I glanced down to see what was causing me excruciating pain and saw that my right leg was facing behind me, was twisted upside down, with the broken femur sticking out.

I suffered numerous broken bones and very nearly bled to death from various deep gashes, particularly around my head and neck. I had seven blood transfusions. But a talented team of trauma surgeons at Grady Memorial Hospital (a charity hospital) frantically worked on me for hours and saved my wretched life.

I was in a coma for some time afterward and in critical condition, but I eventually regained consciousness. My recovery was long and painful, particularly because of my broken right femur, which initially required a 12-hour operation and follow-up surgery.

At this point I should mention that what is described in the next few paragraphs documents the most meaningful experience of my life. It was the tipping point for me, when my life changed dramatically for the better. Some might view it with suspicion or even contempt, but all I can say is that it worked for me and I owe all of the success I've enjoyed to this day to that event. Had it not happened, I truly believe I would be dead or incarcerated in prison, (probably on death row), or in an insane asylum instead of "living the dream."

*Read it objectively, thoughtfully, and decide if it
applies to your walk on this planet too. If so, great; if
not, that is your decision. At any rate, the rest of the
book will not dwell on this life-changing experience,
rather it will detail the important, pragmatic steps I
took afterward to reach the success I have today.*

My recovery was long. To alleviate the sheer boredom of
staring at a hospital ceiling day after day, I started reading
books. I'd been an insomniac for as long as I could
remember and even to this day rarely sleep more than three
to four hours a night. As a kid I developed a passion for
reading just to pass the dark hours.

In the hospital, I'd befriended a nurse named Lydia and
convinced her to check out books for me from the library.
When I reviewed the library's best-seller list, the Bible was
first. I'd never read the Bible because I thought it had been
written by weak people for weak people who were afraid to
die. Since I didn't fear anything or anyone, I had no use for it.

But I was curious. My accident had not changed me or
got me thinking about becoming a follower of God. I just
thought it would be intellectually challenging to read it and
fun to find its flaws, prove it's a fairy tale, and rip to shreds
any Bible-thumping evangelist who later got in my face.

I was no longer an atheist. I'd learned through practicing
witchcraft that a spiritual world existed. As a warlock, I'd
personally seen many supernatural events that weren't mere
coincidence. Consequently, I didn't deny the existence of
God; I just didn't like Him and didn't want anything to do
with Him (aside from maybe asking Him why He was so
mean). I didn't blame myself for my tragic life; I blamed

Him for all of the heartbreaking things that I'd endured.

So I started reading the Bible, beginning with Genesis in the Old Testament. It was incredibly boring with long tedious genealogies: This guy begat that guy and he begat another, and on and on and on. It was so tedious that I very nearly abandoned the project straightaway. I stopped reading and before tossing it aside began thumbing through the New Testament. I noticed some underlined verses with notes scribbled beside them. I smiled as I thought of my nurse, Lydia; this was her personal Bible. I could picture her furrowing her brow and carefully marking the verses she felt were so important that she needed to underline them in order to refer to them at a later time.

I decided to read the New Testament. And as much as I hated to admit it, I was blown away. The more I read, the more my opinion of God changed.

Jesus Christ was nothing like I thought He was!

He spoke of love at every turn, and His love was not bestowed on a few chosen elites and self-righteous religious buffoons, but lavished on anyone and everyone, including criminals like me. He ate and drank with prostitutes, scumbags, drunks, lepers, and ordinary people with real problems. And He did so in spite of all of the pious religious types telling Him not to associate with "sinners." He helped everyone and performed miracle upon miracle.

After I read the four Gospels (Matthew, Mark, Luke, John), I continued through Acts, Romans, and Corinthians. I began thinking I might have been wrong all these years; the Bible and Jesus were nothing like I envisioned them. I really liked Jesus's courage, compassion, and wisdom. I felt closer to Him than anyone I'd ever encountered. Even though I was a grown man, not one person had ever said to me "I love you." But suddenly I realized that Jesus did. Tears filled my eyes, and I quickly wiped them away so no one would see them. Crying was totally out of character for me. I hadn't cried since my early youth, and I believed that it was only for babies, women, and sissies.

As I continued reading, I learned God loved us so much that He willingly allowed His Son to die in our stead and to take the punishment for our sins upon Himself. I was totally intrigued by that. So I kept eagerly reading and soaking it all in, and then I came to Philippians 4:13. It read, *"I can do all things through Christ who strengthens me."*

What? Suddenly, I was **INFURIATED!**

I threw the Bible on the floor, rang for Lydia, and when she appeared I told her to get that Bible out of my sight, that it was nothing but a lie.

Now Lydia was a very large African American woman who was raising five kids and taking care of her sick mother on her own. Numerous freeloading men had treated her shabbily, and her life as a single parent was miserable. She wasn't currently living with a man and didn't want one around "sponging off of her." Additionally, she was a diabetic with high blood pressure and carried the added burden of caring for some of the biggest losers in society in an open ward in a charity hospital.

This day her stress level and blood pressure were out of control, and she was surly, short-tempered, and not in the mood to take any guff from me, (or anyone); especially when I was calling her precious Bible a lie.

She stood over me with her hands on her hips, eyes blazing, and bellowed, *"What are you talking about?"*

Not to be intimidated, I defiantly snarled back through clenched teeth that the Bible said I could do "anything through Christ who strengthens me." I shouted, "But I'm a meth addict. I've worn out the veins in both my arms and now shooting up in my legs. I'm a drunk. I'm a criminal and have done terrible things. I've never done *anything* good in my life. *I can't change!* The only way I'll change is to die and be buried in a $100 pine box in a pauper's grave like so many people I've seen. I can't change, Lydia! It's all a big lie."

She angrily glowered as she put her hands on her big hips and shouted:

"JESUS IS GOD!"

He can do anything He wants! This ain't about **YOU**; it's about **HIM**. He's the One who does the changing of your sorry hide.

He made the blind see.

He cured the lepers.

He walked on water.

He fed 5,000 people with a couple of loaves of bread and a few fish.

And He raised Lazarus from the dead.

And if He can do all that, *He can save your sorry tail!"* (Actually she used a little more colorful language than that.)

She stalked over to her Bible lying on the floor, picked it up and gingerly wiped it off, and set it beside me on the bed. Then she stomped out of my room, huffily snorting and muttering to herself as she went.

I slumped back on my pillow and considered what she'd

said. If God exists, and I now believed He did, and He had created everything that we know (including me), then He could surely change me. That is *if* He wanted to, but that was a big *if*. Why would He want to? I wasn't worth saving.

I started thinking about His death by crucifixion. To start, He was beaten to a bloody pulp. I knew all too well what it looked like to beat someone that badly and could clearly envision Jesus and his wounds. Next, He was mercilessly whipped by Roman soldiers with 39 vicious lashes to His back. Then they yanked out his beard by the roots, and wove razor-sharp thorns into a crude crown and beat it onto His head. In this weakened condition He was forced to carry a heavy cross through the town and up a hillside. All the while, people mocked Him, laughed at Him, and spit in His face.

Finally, when He got to the top of the hill, the soldiers stripped Him, nailed His feet and hands to the wooden cross, and stood it up in front of the blaspheming mob and *in front of His mother.* He struggled to breathe and suffered excruciating pain as he slowly began to die. But as He hung there, He looked down upon those responsible and lovingly said, *"Father forgive them because they know not what they do."*

WHAT?

Had that been me, I would have screamed for God to kill every last one of them—*slowly*. I'd have implored Him to kill their kids first and make them watch. But Jesus was different. He even loved those who were cursing and killing Him. Why would He do such a thing? In the first place, I couldn't understand love, and second, I darn sure couldn't understand Him loving those who were brutally torturing and killing Him.

The story didn't end there and this was the tipping point in changing my life. One of the two criminals being crucified alongside Him started making fun of Jesus. He shouted, "If you're God, then why not save yourself, and while you're at it, save us too?" The other criminal told him to leave Jesus alone, saying they deserved their punishment but that He was innocent and had done nothing wrong. Then he looked at Jesus and asked Him to remember him when He entered His kingdom.

Jesus replied, *"This day you will be in paradise with me."*

WHAT?

Again, I couldn't believe His answer. How could this be? How could this criminal, who was being executed, and who had probably never done anything good in his life, be allowed into heaven? I'd always thought one must do good to get into heaven. Somehow Jesus had changed that. He gave each of us a clean slate. Although I didn't understand it fully, I wanted some of that. I was sick and tired of being sick and tired, and I embraced the possibility that there might be some real hope for me.

I couldn't comprehend why He loved me and why Jesus died a horrid death in order to allow some low life like me into His heaven, and will never understand it, but I knew His love was genuine. God, through Jesus, provided a way for even the worst of the worst, like that criminal and me, to join Him in paradise.

I'd taken copious notes as I read the Bible, and I excitedly went back through them in detail and reviewed certain verses that showed the way to redemption.

I did as each one instructed. I prayed to God. There were verses like,

"For God so loved the world that He gave His only Son that whoever believes in Him will not perish but have everlasting life" – (John 3:16).

I told God that I believed in Jesus.

Then I found these verses regarding my sins:

"For all have sinned and fallen short of the glory of God" – (Romans 3:23).

"The wages (consequences) of sin is death, but the gift of God is eternal life in Christ Jesus" – (Romans 6:23).

"If we confess our sins, He is faithful and just to forgive us our sins, and to cleanse us from all unrighteousness" – (1 John 1:9).

Right there in that hospital bed I told God that I believed in Jesus. I confessed as many of my sins as I could remember and asked to be forgiven. To be honest I was so evil at this point in my life that it was dripping out of my pores, and there were so many sins that I'd committed that I couldn't remember them all, so I asked God to please forgive me for them as well. I *read . . .*

"If you confess with your mouth, 'Jesus is LORD,' and believe in your heart that God raised Him from the dead, you will be saved" – (Romans 10:9).

I confessed with my mouth that Jesus is LORD and that God raised Him from the dead, and I believed it in my heart.

And for the first time in my life I felt a huge burden lift off my shoulders, and then a very warm feeling began coursing up and down my spine, blanketing me in God's love. It was a wonderful feeling, and at that very moment I knew I was saved.

Almost instantly I felt remorse for what I'd become, (something those military psychiatrists told me I was incapable of doing), and now with God's help I wanted to do something good with my life. It was totally out of character for me. I felt determined to change my life for good, and I knew that God would help me to do it.

Since that day I've read the Bible all of the way through so many times I don't even know the count, and hardly a day has gone by that I haven't spent time studying it. When I got out of the hospital, the first thing I did was stop taking drugs and I wouldn't hang with anyone who did. I quit smoking cigarettes. It was a nasty, expensive habit and bad for my health. I'd never really cared about my health, because I doubted that I would live past 25 years. But now my life had changed and I had a reason to live and wanted to clean up my act.

Even though I'd been a hard-core drug user with a big habit and intravenously addicted for years, I was able to get off drugs without going to rehab, AA, NA, or any other support group, (though from what I understand, those are all great programs that have helped millions of suffering people to get sober and stay that way). I just made up my mind to quit, and I did. The hardest thing to stop was the violence. I'd been fighting since I was old enough to make a fist, and changing that behavior was monumentally challenging. Nonetheless, with the exception of a few relatively minor backsliding episodes, I learned to control my hair-trigger temper and suppress the urge to pummel anyone who got in my way.

Next was my battle with alcohol. I'd been an alcoholic since the age of 13, and it was the last vice that I undertook in my effort to get clean. It was very challenging to stop drinking. Illegal-drug use was not as widespread, making it easy enough to avoid people who used them, but it seemed everyone drank alcohol and it was always so tempting. Eventually God found a way to help me and I stopped drinking as well.

I even cut my shoulder-length hair and started wearing nice clothes. I looked like a typical clean-cut college kid, and I told no one of my past. But trying to fit into "straight" society was a monumental task. I'd seen it all (including people die before my eyes). It was tough to put all that out of my mind and not feel different.

I was on crutches for two years and unable to drive at first. But I found a very low-paying job and took a bus to work for a while until a coworker I befriended gave me rides. I lived a solitary life in a tiny apartment without a phone, television, or radio—or any friends or family. And yes, I almost went crazy. After a few months, I bought a relic of a car. Sometimes it started, and sometimes it didn't.

One night I went to a disco near my apartment and met a nice girl from a good family. She was nothing like me. She'd lived in the same house all her life in a home full of love. She was a Goody Two-Shoes. She didn't do drugs, drink to excess, and definitely wasn't wild. Her family went on camping trips together, decorated the Christmas tree together, and cooked big Sunday dinners together. Everything together. I didn't tell her about my past because I was ashamed and didn't want to scare her off. When she asked, I told her I didn't want to discuss it because it was too painful. (Actually, I didn't tell her much about my past for *14 years*.) She seemed perfect for me, primarily because she was stable and sane. I still had deep emotional scars, anger issues, and drugs had scrambled my mind. To this day it is still tough to forget the years of abuse, anger, violence, resentment, and bitterness, not to mention the addictions—ingesting massive amounts of drugs and alcohol—and the crazy experiences.

I definitely needed stability and normalcy in my life, and she was the picture of normalcy. We were nearly opposites, but as far as I was concerned that was a good thing. Three months after we met I asked her to marry me, and she accepted.

I landed my first real job at Glidden, a paint manufacturing plant. I lied about my employment history and criminal record in order to land the worst-paying job in the entire plant of some 400 people. I knew the only way I could get ahead was to be the first at work and the last to leave, to volunteer for whatever miserable task no one else wanted to do, and to work harder and smarter than everyone else. For $350 a month, Glidden sent me into the bowels of the plant, into a dark, filthy, dank "hole" where I performed my job of keeping up with the labels for the cans of paint.

I was not resentful that I started at the bottom; I was thankful to be employed. Had Glidden checked my résumé, I'd never have been hired; I was still wanted in three states.

So I cleaned the grimy room from top to bottom. I organized the labels and painted the floors, walls, and ceiling white. And for a six-pack of beer I bribed a maintenance guy to install fluorescent lights every six inches across the ceiling. Soon enough, my little label room was lit up like Times Square.

While making these changes to my dark room, I also faced a different challenge. I was sorely tempted to knock out the teeth of my immediate supervisor on a daily basis. He was a sawed-off shrimp with a big mouth, and he liked to yell. It was all I could do to keep from sending him to the hospital. I was tempted to quit many times and go back to a life of crime. I knew I could make more money in five minutes on the street than in an entire month in this godforsaken place.

All I had to do was put a gun in someone's face and take his money. I asked God to help me during these times, bit my lip, kept my head down, and just kept working.

My hard work began to pay off. The transformation of the label department was obvious to all who walked by it; however, what really caught the plant manager's attention were my new changes that saved the company some very significant money on paint labels. He was genuinely appreciative of my work ethic, and even more, the excellent cost-cutting programs that I developed. He was so impressed that he had me promoted to the inventory control and distribution department where I did essentially the same thing by increasing efficiency and cutting costs. As before, I was quickly promoted and given more responsibility.

I was promoted eight times, right to a position on the elite plant management team, and the only one without a college degree. That was a great day for me, but not so great for that punk supervisor who had seemed to delight in bossing me around when I had worked in the label room. Now I was *his* boss, and though I'm positive Jesus would have forgiven him, I wasn't that advanced in the love-all-serve-all category. I made his life far more miserable than he'd ever made mine, and I enjoyed every minute of it.

At this time, computers were just coming into business use, and commercial software had not yet been developed. If a company like Glidden wanted to computerize its operation it had to write its own software from a rudimentary code (by today's standards).

Glidden had purchased an IBM mainframe computer and hired several programmers to design a custom software system for its manufacturing and distribution systems. Since I'd worked in virtually every department in the plant, including being a "roving supervisor" and covering for any manager on any shift anywhere in the operation, I was selected to help the programmers understand how things worked through the various departments. This experience proved invaluable. I learned how software functioned and how to successfully implement it. (Later on, when I began building my own companies, software was still unavailable commercially, so I designed my own systems and hired programmers to write code for them. I eventually formed a software company and made millions selling the technology I'd innovated.)

Not long after this project, I considered starting a business. I was confident I could do it and excited about the prospect of working for myself. But when I mentioned it to a few friends and family members I was immediately bombarded with negativity.

"You can't start a company."

"You don't have any money."

"You've never owned a business and have zero experience."

"You have no education."

"I mean, *really*. Who do you think you are anyway?"

"You're going to give up a job paying $30,000 a year to start a company at no salary. Are you *crazy*? Let me answer that for you, yes you are *crazy!*"

It all sounded identical to what I'd heard my entire life: "You're stupid." "You'll never amount to anything." "You're a black sheep." "You're a bad seed." "You **CAN'T**." "You **CAN'T**." "You **CAN'T!**"

Grrr!

You want to know what I told every last one of them?

"I **CAN** do all things through Christ who strengthens me!" Philippians 4:13 had become my life's verse. I believed it, and I believed in myself, even if no one else did, including my wife.

I was an airbrush artist and creating art with it was my hobby, and I'd noticed that the only paints available at the time were automotive lacquers for automobiles. They were totally unsuitable for art.

I asked my chemist friends from the paint industry to suggest a way to formulate an airbrush paint system that matched my design criteria. I started a little paint business in my basement. I spent untold hours developing the colors I wanted and experimenting with various resins and pigments until I perfected the technology. When I finished, it was outstanding, and as testimony, the top airbrush artist in the country became my biggest promoter. So I quit my job, borrowed $1,000 on my credit card to start my first business, and "jumped out of the airplane with no parachute."

As it turned out, the system I developed (Polytranspar) was a technological breakthrough. It's still the best airbrush paint of its kind worldwide and has won too many competitions to count. About six months after founding the company, it was a multimillion-dollar business with some 286,000 customers and seven worldwide distributers. I went from netting $30K a year to $30K a *week*.

I was on fire, and it was as though I knew how to feed this flame. I added products as fast as I could, using the proceeds to expand into areas such as manufacturing, distribution, and video production; I started a mail-order company and published a world-class magazine and books; opened retail stores and produced public events; and did consulting and software development. The list went on. In the early days I worked 20 hours a day, six and seven days a week. All the effort paid off.

One day I was looking at my financials and realized I had a net worth of over $1 million. I was a millionaire—at age 35! I had reached society's definition of the pinnacle of success in just a few short years through my faith in Jesus Christ, hard work, smart choices, and perseverance.

I went on to found 19 successful businesses. I guess

those military shrinks were wrong. I became a *serial entrepreneur* instead of a *serial killer.*

In 2008 I sold my largest and most successful enterprise, Horizon Software International LLC, an institutionalized-food-service software-technology company, for $75 million. My cash deal had no debt, no partners (other than my children), and I didn't have to serve as a board member or consultant. I just left with a wheelbarrow full of money, grinning like a crazy old fox.

Horizon was a blue-ribbon software-development company. Our software system revolutionized the institutionalized-food-service industry with innovative ideas and user-friendly design. We had over 18,000 installations worldwide, servicing public schools, hospitals, retirement communities, prisons, and the Department of Defense, including every land base, ship, submarine, and remote battlefield for the U.S. Army, Navy, Marine Corp, and Air Force. (Not too shabby for someone drummed out of military service!)

My last business venture involved the development of multimillion-dollar Honey Lake Resort and Spa, built on my sprawling 4,800-acre quail-hunting plantation near Tallahassee, Florida. We hosted weddings, spiritual and corporate retreats, hunting parties, and individuals who just wanted to enjoy the park-like beauty of this gorgeous place with its dazzling, spring-fed, 80-acre lake. I bought the property in 2008 and opened for business in 2010. I recently sold the resort and some acreage to a megachurch in Jacksonville, Florida.

A couple of months ago I cofounded my 20th business, a

joint venture with my coauthor Jamie Vrinios. The company is called *Jesus Take the Lead*. It's dedicated to developing DVDs and books such as this one, and providing live coaching, teaching programs, and inspirational speaking engagements. Our goal is to share what we've learned with others who want to become successful and attain their dreams.

Through the years I've received many awards and national acclaim for my business acumen. I was selected from among hundreds of contestants in Atlanta, as the Gwinnett County Chamber of Commerce (third largest in the country) Business Person of the Year. I was also a finalist for the Atlanta Ernst and Young Entrepreneur of the Year Award, which was previously won by distinguished industry leaders like Michael Dell of Dell Computers.

My companies were recognized by INC. magazine as being among the most successful in the nation, and I was a keynote speaker at INC.'s annual awards ceremony in Washington, D.C. I was featured in *Florida Trend, Business Week, Investor's Business Daily, The Christian Post, Reader's Digest, Forbes*, on AOL, MSNBC, Yahoo, and in various newspaper articles from around the globe like a front-page newspaper article in Athens, Greece (I couldn't read a word of it and now I understand the meaning of "It's Greek to me."). There are too many publications to remember, plus the hundreds of radio and television interviews.

All of this attention and for sure the millions of dollars and the toys that followed were all well and good. But aside from my personal walk with the Lord, my proudest achievement has been raising a great family. My sons love the Lord as well. They excelled in every sport while growing up, and we went camping, water skiing, hunting, and fishing together as often as possible. They learned to love God's great outdoors like I do.

My family has worked with me in every business I've owned, and I taught them everything I could. My sons all graduated from college with excellent scholastic achievements, and they work hard and smart. Today, all three are very successful businessmen in their own right and are making their mark on the world. They are genuinely happy, and most important is that they love their children with all their hearts, and are married to godly women whom they deeply love.

Despite how it may look, life has not always been easy for me since my transformation. I suffered through the loss of my brother's son to a brain tumor. A few years later my brother committed suicide. My mother died of a brain tumor. I had nearly a million dollars embezzled from me, and I narrowly escaped bankruptcy because of it.

Just because you follow God and/or have millions of dollars does not mean you are excluded from the world's pain. A strong relationship with God enabled me to live through the heartache of all this tragedy.

One more story: Once I got a taste of success, I became infatuated with making mega amounts of money and collecting material things. Success was another thing I became addicted to, and like many people it very nearly destroyed me. At one point I owned 15 cars and five houses. I dressed in silk shirts unbuttoned halfway down my chest to expose the gaudy gold chain and medallion hanging around my neck. I wore Gucci shoes and skintight pants and strutted around like a peacock. I roared around in a red convertible Porsche with the top down.

I looked like a pimp.

Fortunately, I came to my senses and realized that all material things are temporary and as King Solomon said, "meaningless" and "vanity." I learned that what's really important is to have peace, joy, and love in your life. Most important, I discovered I could not attain these life treasures apart from God. I've lived a full life and sampled just about everything (both good and bad), and I can honestly say there is nothing that satisfies apart from a relationship with Jesus.

When I started my career, I needed a mentor. I asked myself, "If I could have anyone in the world, who would it be?" Of course I thought of Jesus first, but then I remembered King Solomon. The Bible states that he was the richest and wisest man who ever lived or will live.

I developed the mission statement for my first company using Jesus as my example. I thought of the various aspects of a business and asked myself what Jesus would do.

He came to serve, and that prompted me to write the first plank:

To provide OUTSTANDING customer service.

Then I wondered about the products or service He might offer. My second plank became:

To provide products of the highest quality possible.

I followed with pricing:

To offer fair prices; fair to the consumer, fair to me, our employees, and our company.

Finally, I thought about interaction with others, which put in place my final plank:

To work together with honesty, integrity, and treat everyone, including consumers, employees, and vendors, as we would like to be treated.

Every company I owned has had this same mission statement, and I strictly enforced it. I was particularly obsessed with customer service. If someone treated one of my valued customers shabbily, "heads would roll."

This mission statement works exceedingly well, and I highly recommend it.

Once I had that foundation in place, I turned to old King Solomon. I read Proverbs (the book of wisdom) so many times I nearly memorized it, and I also read Ecclesiastes with fervor. (He wrote both books.) I researched everything I could find that had any information about him. I learned from his triumphs and failures. I even visited Israel with $25,000 in camera equipment, primarily to record all of the wonders created by Solomon. I wanted to see the vineyards, the palaces, the stables, and all his great works. But when I got there, it was rubble and covered in vines.

This made me realize that building an earthly empire was all vanity, just as he'd said. Eventually, all will be reduced to ruins. I thought of the buildings and great companies that I'd constructed. I envisioned them in 200 years, demolished and deserted. It was an eye-opening experience to discover that this life is truly a mere vapor, just as the Bible states. We live an average of 79.9 years on earth, but eternity is FOREVER! I realized I should be an "eternity thinker," focusing more on becoming a part of building God's heavenly kingdom than my earthly one. A kingdom that would never be in ruins, not like my earthly version that would ultimately become rubble and dust.

Today I've surrendered everything to the Lord and am still completely drug- and alcohol-free. I'm no longer a slave to the "flash and the cash," the pride of life, and the lust for unadulterated power and material things. What is important to me now is giving back.

I've spent much of my free time over the past several decades sharing my life story in an effort to provide hope to those who need it. I tell anyone who will listen that I started at rock bottom but rose to success through my faith in Jesus Christ, and I give Him all of the credit.

I write an encouraging devotional five days a week entitled *Words for the Day* (*www.wordsfortheday.org*). I've been doing this for the past 18 years. I currently serve on the board of directors for Inmate Encounter Prison Ministry and previously served on the Bill Glass Behind the Walls Prison Ministry board. I founded, built, and attend Honey Lake Church and Worldwide Ministries in Greenville, Florida. I also firmly believe in philanthropy, although I find that God out-gives me without exception.

In 2012 God began revealing Himself to me, and I felt a calling to lead an effort to unite the body of believers globally and develop a worldwide communications network to equip, connect, and motivate people to spread the good news of the Gospel.

Once I received God's call, I immediately founded The Jesus Alliance (*www.jesusalliance.org*). I divested myself of all business interests in which I had an active role except those that directly helped further the vision of the Alliance. Currently, I work full-time as its founder, chairman, and CEO.

I have much more to say about how you, too, can find success regardless of the situation you're in. But it's time for Jamie to share her story.

BOB WILLIAMSON AND JAMIE VRINIOS

CHAPTER 1

Long Shots

Jamie Vrinios

Let me ask you a question. What are the odds a recently divorced 21-year-old single mom of two children under the age of two, who was disowned by her parents and family living on government funding, would rise to put her children through college, develop a multimillion-dollar business, become a top national sales director, write a best-selling book, speak all over the world to hundreds of thousands of people, and ultimately be living the life of her dreams 30 years later?

Be honest, you never would have given that woman a chance. But that woman is me. I faced that dark period in my life as a young woman, and, yes, I was afraid, but I discovered how to be BRAVE. I pushed through my fears again and again, and against all odds I succeeded beyond expectations.

Many people give into fear when they find themselves in a dark space of life, especially if they desire to pursue an outrageous dream; however, I've learned that we must confront fear. That is why all great beginnings are brave.

Can you imagine the thoughts running through my mind at such a young age? I can tell you that when I found myself alone and afraid with absolutely no family to help support me, or even give me so much as a dime, it was hard to believe in myself, much less in my dreams. But you know what? I made a decision to rise up and fight. So many times people base their decisions on how they feel. My "feelings" were irrelevant, because I had two children, whom I loved with all my heart, counting on me. Their futures were nonnegotiable.

I'm often asked how I pushed through those dark days, and the answer is simple: Every time I looked at my children's sweet faces I knew that I had to *fight* for them. There was no option. The decisions I made to get up again and again after being knocked down were easy to make. I simply had to do whatever was best for my children, pure and simple! My son and daughter were always my inspiration and I was determined to make sure they would never experience the abuse, hate, and rejection I encountered as a child and scared teenage mom.

My brave beginning started out when I had absolutely nothing and was on government assistance. Living in poverty was heartbreaking when it came to my children, because I desperately wanted to give them everything they wanted. My biggest fear was losing them because I couldn't provide a quality life. So I was looking everywhere for opportunities to make money. I am grateful to this day for government assistance; however, there was no way I was going to stay on it.

I wanted more for my children than just "surviving" and hoping we could make ends meet. The humiliation of being at the grocery checkout and having to put back food my children wanted because I didn't have enough money reminded me that I MUST FIGHT with all of my MIGHT to break out of this poverty lifestyle. I can vividly remember standing in line at the grocery store and feeling the glares from those few hateful people who got angry as I counted out every single penny. My children would cling to me, one on each leg, out of fear and confusion as they wondered why others treated us this way.

Today when I'm in the checkout line and observe a mom who is flat broke, agonizing the same way I did, I want to encourage her to dream of better things and to never give up. I see the embarrassment in her eyes as she apologizes to the impatient people behind her for the longer time it's taking to ring out with food stamps. My heart ached the same way, but I knew deep down there was more to life and that I needed to break free of limited thinking to find it.

Being trapped in abject poverty was frightening. On many occasions the utility company shut off my power in freezing weather. My phone was turned off too. But I just put my head down and kept on working with every ounce of strength I had. I'd never experienced deprivation prior to being disowned. I was raised in a family with more than enough money. My father was a physician and was wealthy, so poverty was quite a shock to me. The irony was that when I was growing up our family had money and all that it brought; however, when it came to living in an environment of love, we were definitely impoverished.

As a little girl, I lived in daily fear because I never knew what was going to happen at home. I was the youngest of six children, and my experiences as a child were not what I would define as "Brady Bunch" memories. To the outside world we were the "perfect family," but that was not the world inside our house. It was more like a nightmarish prison filled with abuse, fear, and hatred.

Many in such circumstances grow up to hate themselves and deem themselves worthless, and I was no exception. I was living proof of this vicious cycle. As a child my self-esteem was destroyed, and I yearned to have someone love me. The self-hatred I felt led me to believe I was so ugly that I actually bleached my skin to remove the freckles from my body.

I hope by now you understand that even though I was cut off by my wealthy family as a young mom with two small children, my meager new home was richer in love than I'd experienced in my entire life. I'd learned firsthand that you can have all the money in the world, but if you don't have love, you have nothing.

At this time in my life, the portrait I had of myself was of worthlessness, and that is by far the most difficult obstacle I've ever had to overcome. I want you to know that even to this day I remind myself daily that I am absolutely worthy of the very best that life has to offer, and you should do the same for yourself starting right now.

So there I was feeling worthless, and one look at my financial situation verified that I was right in that regard. The world would have likewise declared that this young single mom of two was going to be another statistic of failure, but I knew I could beat the odds, and I totally refused to lose.

It was at this point that I started picking up various jobs and pursuing a degree in respiratory therapy. I worked long hours and went without sleep most nights to create a better life for my children. I attended class in the morning and babysat for friends and neighbors during the afternoon but it still wasn't enough income. I knew I had to find another job.

One day I arranged to meet with the head of the physical education department at a local junior college. I had to be persistent to get a few minutes of his time. I believed I could get the job even though I had no prior experience or education. The only thing I knew was that I could dance well enough to create an aerobics class that would attract a following. I loved working out so why not get paid for it. My schedule was full during the day, but my evenings were free. He asked why he should hire me, and I told him there would be a waiting list to take my aerobics classes. I guess that convinced him, because he offered me a job. I ended up teaching physical education classes in various towns on different nights because it was the best money I could make at the time and I went anywhere I was needed. I became so thin from all the teaching and stress that I stopped menstruating, but I kept at it.

My schedule was extreme and I went with very little sleep but I did what I had to do as I was finishing my degree. I just kept telling myself it was going to be ok and that my situation was only temporary. It was difficult getting through school with two children and no support but I was fortunate enough to have a professor who was empathetic to my situation. He was the head of the respiratory therapy department and helped me tremendously. There were many times where I had to bring my children with me to school due to unforeseen circumstances and he would let them stay in his office while I took my exams. God has always placed people in my life along the way to help me and he was one of them early on that was pivotal to my success in school.

I am extremely grateful for that professor because he was my sole support during this time. In fact, when I finally graduated, he and my children were the only ones by my side. After that, I stopped babysitting and went into respiratory therapy full time. The passion I felt to give my children a bright future became my obsession.

Some people have judged me regarding this ambition; however, they have never walked in my shoes and I have zero regrets as I look back. As a single mom I worked as many night shifts available at the hospital as a therapist so my days would be open for my children. I worked every single holiday because the pay was twice as much. The holidays were the hardest for me and suicidal thoughts were there, especially because I never received invitations to come visit my family members.

The picture of worthlessness would rush into my mind, so I compensated by throwing myself into work and trying my utmost to help the people in those hospital beds. During the loneliest periods, when I even entertained thoughts of suicide, I learned that the more I helped others the more I helped myself. There are always people who have it much worse. It is our choice to dream and live, or doubt and die, and I chose to LIVE.

I learned to rise up rather than give up, and instead of being ashamed of my scars they gradually became reminders of what I'd overcome and my inspiration to go on. Eventually, I came to see that the battles we win in life are not just about us; they're about inspiring others and helping them win too.

I continued working nights as a therapist, but I was

barely making enough money to provide any kind of future for my children. And there was so much more I dreamed about than living paycheck to paycheck. Although I wasn't sure how I could ever be anything beyond a therapist, I was OPEN to more.

And then an opportunity presented itself.

I was invited to a conference in Chicago, where a door opened for me. I met a man who offered me a job in medical sales even though I had zero experience, and I said yes.

This move would give me an opportunity to make a transformation in my life and would usher in another brave beginning. I can tell you that every single time we go to a new level in life we must allow ourselves to go through the transformational process and begin again.

My experience in working with countless leaders has shown me that very few will ever want to go through this transformation, because they are afraid of the side effects along the way. You may wonder what I mean. Every time we go to a new phase of life we will have to say good-bye to the familiar and, in many cases, declare war on the things that can prevent us from moving forward.

TRUTH: the majority of people refuse to let go of the past in order to embrace the NEW.

I was more than ready to unleash the new into my life, so I said yes to a job offer in medical sales that would require me to move to Chicago. Here I was, living in a town of just 2,000, and now I would move my children to Chicago, with zero experience in sales and no guarantee of success.

WOW! is right, and YES, I was afraid, but I knew I had to spread my wings and FLY. I remember walking into the hospital and saying good-bye to everyone as they reminded me that I would be back, but I knew that there was never going to be any turning back. When we are truly ready to transform we are willing to eliminate the other options: Reverting to the caterpillar state of crawling when we have already metamorphosed into a butterfly is just not possible.

I remember the day we moved to Chicago as a HUGE marker in my life, and I knew on that day that it would require more determination than ever if I were to succeed. We drove to Wheaton, Illinois, and moved into a townhome that cost $1,000 a month, five times what I was paying in my small town. We can never be successful without leaving our comfort zones, and I assure you I was clearly out of my comfort zone. The first day of work I was handed a map of DuPage and Cook counties and told that this would be my territory, and then I was asked if I had any questions. I had a small base salary and the rest was commission, so if my quotas weren't met my bills would not get paid. Standing there with those maps in my hand, I thought what a huge mistake I'd made, but that was just fear. I'd committed to never going back, so I had to move forward.

Every day I fought traffic for hours to visit hospitals in these counties. Often I'd park and start walking to the account only to lose my nerve, turn back, and go sit in the car, wondering what the heck I was going to say and how in the world I would ever succeed at this. To make matters harder, I was also working as an on-call respiratory therapist.

We would have weekly sales meetings and my boss

would ask me how things were going, and I would nod and reply how awesome things were. My job would be gone if I didn't produce, so I finally started calling on doctors and building the relationships that would lead to great results. I had no sales experience, but I learned that it was less about "sales" and more about meeting the needs of my clients and forming a business network. I was making sales calls during the day and was on call at night as a therapist. It was not uncommon for me to be paged in the middle of the night to go to a place in downtown Chicago. It was a crazy life, and sometimes I'd have to drive to the most impoverished areas of Chicago to do things like replace a sleep apnea monitor that had been sold for drugs.

I saw it all during these calls. Among the experiences was seeing a mother strung out on drugs and her tiny baby addicted to cocaine. It was heart wrenching, and a stark reminder of how grateful I was to have conquered those dark moments of worthlessness that could have left me living this exact life of pain and poverty. So many times in dark moments we may want to give up, but we must be determined to RISE. My obsession to never go back grew stronger the more I was exposed to these living conditions, and my passion to make a difference in this life became crystal clear.

My commissions started increasing, and my confidence grew. I pushed through the rejection that was a daily part of the job in a sales career. I am sure you can understand that after being disowned and ignored by your parents and family for years, rejection by strangers seems minor in comparison. The scars I'd carried from my family's hatred and indifference served me well in my career. My children were my life, and every penny I made was put toward their needs. My income was considered good; however, the custody battles with my ex-husband's wealthy family for my children were never ending, so we were still living paycheck to paycheck.

The self-imposed guilt trips a single mom carries along with the labels placed on her by society are painful. Many teachers at my children's school judged and even condemned me as they observed me from their limited point of view. My children and I were put into these special categories designed just for single moms who can't be at all the school activities. The naysayers were all around me, and it only fueled the fire inside of me even more to beat the odds. Many will quit when the obstacles seem insurmountable, but the few who are crazy enough to pursue their outrageous dreams with all they have will live life to its fullest.

The past 24 years I've had the opportunity to lead a sales team of thousands, and it is through working with these leaders that I can say with certainty that there are FEW who have the confidence to ignore the negative people, but those who do can realize their dreams in short order. I believe this strength arises from the vision we have from the beginning. I had a vision of a better life, so instead of focusing on what was in front of me, I continued to play the commercials in my mind of what I saw in the future. I refused to feed my children or myself the oh-so-common diet of giving up on those dreams that many forces on the outside encouraged me to do daily. When you've come to that point of firmly deciding on a goal, the methodology will follow, and you just figure it out. Keep in mind, it is the end of the rainbow that we must focus on, and not what we go through to get there. Yep, the small-minded people of the world will throw insults at your dream, so just remember you are not alone in this and, by the way you, are in great company.

We are a summation of the voices we listen to the most, so the question becomes what voices will you allow into your dream? The voice of TRUTH or the deadly words of discouragement. The people you surround yourself with will impact your decision to fight or agree with the excuses you may use in order to give up. I refused to listen to all the naysayers and continued to climb regardless of the rocks thrown my way—and, in fact, I used them to build my future! I put in long hours as a sales rep and was considered a valuable player in the medical company I worked for; however, that was about to end and I did not see it coming. The door on this job was about to shut and I would be faced with another brave beginning very soon.

One day I was fortunate enough to be approached by another company while I was calling on some doctors at MacNeal Hospital in Berwyn IL. I was literally on the pay phone in the lobby of the hospital when I met two female medical reps who would open another door of possibilities. We immediately connected and they asked if I could meet with the head of marketing the next week and of course I said yes without hesitation.

I will never forget the interview because I woke up that morning with strep throat and a high fever. There was absolutely nothing however, that could have prevented me from making my appointment that day. I so badly wanted to succeed, I looked at being sick as being irrelevant and a mere inconvenience. Despite being very ill the interview was flawless and that company immediately hired me for a marketing position and territory that covered five states. The funny thing...I did not have a degree in marketing and knew nothing about how to do the job. But you know what? I was willing to take a risk, and the company was too.

I believe if you want to succeed WILDLY, taking risks in life is a MUST. I was soaring with this new company, but there was something missing. I was not fulfilled. Have you ever felt like that? I was traveling every other week to various states, packing two weeks of work into one and making great money, but I had no passion for what I was doing. I found myself back in the same mind-set I had as a therapist, working and wondering if this is all there is. The pursuit of money without purpose is a shallow existence, and I had signed up for the ride. My existence had slowly morphed into a robotic lifestyle, and my passion for life was slowly fading due to lack of vision to see past my corporate cage.

Do you know that when you put a lion in a cage for any extended period of time it will prefer to stay in the cage instead of the outdoors? In fact, the lion will begin to live comfortably in the cage even though it goes against its instincts. It's a slow kill. So at this point in my life I was definitely in my cage and had even decorated it with nice things, but my spirit just couldn't accept it as my truth and purpose in life. I remember so clearly the day my gut started to question my placement with this company. Was I in the job of my dreams or just existing in a cage?

One day a coworker flew to Chicago to meet some of

the hospital administrators I'd been working with to land an account. What happened next opened my eyes. I will never forget that as we were driving to the hospital she began asking me client details, and as we walked through the doors she removed her wedding ring and said, "Jamie, there is nothing I won't do to get this account." The moment this happened I knew that if anyone asked me to compromise my convictions that would be the day I quit.

Soon after this exchange with my coworker I was in fact put in a very uncomfortable position and lost my job because I refused to compromise my moral standards.

Many people may feel comfortable making money by playing the games that I observed constantly; however, I was not about to enlist in the madness. I will never forget my abrupt dismissal soon after I refused to go against my convictions. I was told my position was being eliminated and the company was restructuring. The time I'd invested in someone else's dream was now gone. I would never regain the time I'd spent, but the lessons I learned were invaluable for my future.

The door of my cage was now open, and I had a choice to either run free or return to the survival mind-set I'd once adapted. At this stage in my life the feeling of worthlessness resurfaced and the reality of possibly losing my children became pronounced because I was spending what extra money I had on attorney fees to keep custody of them. I was in serious financial straits, and the portrait of worthlessness led me to explore every religion I could find; still there was a void.

I was raised in the church, but after my family and our church turned their back on my children and me, I wanted nothing to do with their hypocrisy. My opinion was tainted by my childhood experiences, and I was determined to decide for myself what I believed. I had always trusted in God and knew deep down He had His hand on me, and my children, and I drew my strength from this; however, I waivered constantly in my faith, trying one brand of religion and then another. The condemnation I'd carried through my life was wearing on me, and I couldn't reconcile how God allowed me to experience such pain. I knew deep down God loved me, but at least for the moment I was concerned. What I couldn't know then was that my life was headed for a metamorphosis and dramatic transformation (specifically, my faith). The new portrait I would paint of myself, after years of being haunted with thoughts of worthlessness, would soon begin to appear.

I was determined never to be controlled or manipulated by the corporate world again. I made the decision to begin a business in direct sales with Mary Kay Cosmetics. Months prior to losing my job, I'd been approached by a beautiful woman who'd earned a career car and was thriving as an independent consultant, while still pursuing her career as an architect. I will never forget the day we had a chance meeting on an elevator at West Suburban Hospital in Oak Park, Illinois. Who would have thought that this encounter would change my life forever? I called her soon after I lost my job and told her I wanted to sign up as an independent consultant. The day I called her became the beginning of a life-altering transformation that would lead me to achieve my crazy, awe-inspiring dreams.

At this point I was $100,000 in debt from all the attorney

fees that had been building up, but I was determined to win no matter what. I was feeling braver than ever about this new opportunity, because for the first time in my life I had the love and support around me that had been missing my entire life. In the beginning, I was skeptical and very guarded—it was so new for me and completely opposite of my experiences in corporate America. I made a decision to go from the medical field to cosmetics, and as expected, many of my corporate peers thought I was crazy. If you are serious about pursuing your dream the last thing you ever want to do is enlist public opinion. The "herd" will never understand your passion to live outside of the status quo, and that is why they continue to decorate their cages with disbelief and small thinking.

I stopped putting my dreams in small spaces and threw away the rule book that was holding me back from achieving my greatest potential. My decision to embrace this new business opportunity was the wind beneath my wings that would lift me to places beyond anything I had ever dreamed or imagined.

I moved very swiftly from consultant to a top director and debuted as a national sales director just 9 1/2 years after signing my agreement. My organization consists of thousands of leaders nationally who have joined me in this "cage-free" pursuit of their "crazy" dreams.

There was so much growth in initially building my business that as a young woman it could have hindered me greatly. But I was fortunate enough to meet a mentor who would encourage me along the way. Marilyn Welle was a national sales director with Mary Kay. It's hard to find the words to express how grateful I am to her and for the lessons she taught me about myself and the world.

My transformation began in earnest the very first day we spoke, as she poured love, confidence, and belief into me over the phone. She told me over and over that there is no fear in love and where there is perfect love, miracles happen.

This was a huge moment for me. Marilyn, a total stranger, was not only "reading my personal mail," but also accepting everything she'd discovered about me. She reminded me that "we are only as sick as the secrets we keep," and I had been storing up secrets for years like a chipmunk. For the first time, I began to trust someone. I believed Marilyn when she said there was nothing I could ever do to lose her love and support. She gave me permission to forgive myself and release the past so I could embrace the future. When I got her call I was living in fear due to an abusive ex who had been stalking me almost the entire first year of my business. I'm sure from the outside I looked like the biggest failure there was on all fronts, but on the inside I just kept fighting and believing in a better life.

I was terrified of unpacking all the things that had happened in my life for fear of being judged or misunderstood. Today I talk to women daily and can sense that same fear in their voices so similar to those I owned some 24 years ago, and it is a stark reminder that I need to be that encouraging voice to them, just as Marilyn was to me.

The lessons I learned from her are now being passed down to countless women because she took a chance on this disowned, young, single mom. The pure belief and love she poured into my life ignited a passion inside of me to empower those around me to win. My faith strengthened with every step I took, and my self-portrait began to change into something beautiful. The environment I was swathed in had the perfect elements for me to succeed. I believe that God brought Marilyn into my life to help me evolve from that crawling caterpillar into a winged butterfly, and a new beginning in my life. I knew there would be no more crawling after meeting Marilyn, and besides, it's impossible for a butterfly to turn back into a caterpillar.

After our phone call, I was even more committed to getting a grip on my life, and I decided to check out church again. Many successful business mentors and associates were succeeding by putting God first, so I thought if it was working for them, why not me? I'd tried it my way and had achieved some success, but my dreams were huge. I was open to the advice of those successful people around me who had made God their number one priority. I'd always been told that if you want to be successful in life follow the advice of those who are, and that is exactly what I did.

I will never forget the Sunday morning when my relationship with God took on a completely new meaning. You see, until I walked through the doors of this church, I had been living under self-condemnation and didn't feel I was worthy of God's blessings in my life. I would play the past over and over again in my mind and didn't like what I saw. The very fact that my family had disowned my children and me was something that consistently affirmed the orphan image with which I had been living my entire life. In my heart and mind, I'd enlisted myself into an orphanage and had never even known it until I understood the love story of Jesus Christ. I was raised in the church but never understood the true love and grace of Jesus. I was under the mistaken impression that I had to meet all these "biblical rules" in order to have a relationship with God, so I assumed I would definitely be excluded because of my history.

I accepted Christ as my Lord and Savior and was baptized at 11 years of age but I never actually understood from that point forward God looked at me as *His* daughter. When I was a little girl I would pray every night for God to remove my father or me from my home and couldn't understand why my prayers were never answered.

The ministers that I met that day, including Pastor Grogan, ultimately brought much revelation to me regarding my unanswered questions. The day I walked into the church a man was playing a piano, and his music touched me in a way I'd never experienced before. I was moved to my core and started crying. God began to minister to me through Michael Day and his wife Rena. They had produced Gold records in the secular market and were famous, so I was dumbfounded to see them in church singing and playing music for God. This couple, along with Pastor Grogan, would ultimately play a vital role in my spiritual growth.

My Heavenly Father is the only Father I have known in my life since the age of 19. I'd never truly understood grace or that God loved me unconditionally and saw me as His child. So many questions I had were answered that morning, and a new self-portrait came to light when I finally understood how I was viewed through my Heavenly Father's eyes, and not the eyes of other people. I will never forget the peace that entered my heart and spirit the minute I fully embraced that love and grace of Jesus Christ. I was a daughter of a King and my braver-than-ever beginning was birthed that Sunday morning.

I left there with my spirit on fire, and my vision to make a positive difference in the lives around me was now abundantly clear. The words that Marilyn had spoken over the phone about love were echoed that Sunday: *Where there is perfect love there is no fear.*

I put all my condemnation, rejection, guilt and pain in God's hands that day and embraced another new beginning. Thanks to my newfound relationship with my Father in Heaven, I was feeling more confident than ever as a young entrepreneur, and every conversation I had with Marilyn increased my faith tremendously.

My business began moving at an accelerated pace, and my team of women produced $650,000 in retail sales that year. That foundation built in those early days has led to many multi-millions in retail sales over the past 24 years. Michael, Rena, and Pastor Grogan were pivotal in helping me grow in my walk with the Lord. They were a constant encouragement to me and to the leaders in my organization, and my life had begun to take on an entirely different meaning. I was leading as a top director and earned my first all-expenses-paid luxury trip abroad to Paris, followed by 22 more trips around the world.

I married Peter that year and soon gave birth to my son, Sam, and my business continued to increase dramatically. The passion for my dream never diminished in the least, even after my third child. In fact, it was increasing daily.

I remember at first feeling guilty about my success and the income I was making. There were people around me that said it wasn't Godly for me to be this successful or to have this kind of income. I will never forget my pastor visiting me shortly after Sammy was born, and that particular day I was feeling discouraged about my good fortune. (Can you imagine that?) Pastor Grogan looked me in the eyes and told me that God trusted me with what He had given me and that He would continue to bless me and that I should ignore those around me that said otherwise.

This reinforced my confidence to keep working toward my dreams. I wanted more than anything to provide my family with everything I never had and to help others do the same. My vision of creating a home with limitless thinking and unconditional love solidified as my priority.

The passion I now have for helping others succeed is an addiction that grows stronger daily. I love to see the "long shots" in this world rise up and overcome the odds. There is nothing more rewarding than helping others achieve their dreams.

My children, Nathan, Amber, and Sam, are all successful entrepreneurs and are driven to make a positive contribution to this world. I believe the success of all three of my adult children is without question a result of the example I ingrained in them as they watched me pursue dreams that early on were perceived as "crazy" by so many naysayers.

Today I feel as though I'm just now getting started. I've learned and believe that more is "caught than taught," and my children observed their mom work many long hours to provide them a bright future. I have always been unapologetic about my faith in Jesus Christ, my work ethic, and passion to help others win. I believe the most important lessons I have passed on to my children and others is that God loves us and He has a purpose and plan for our lives and it involves giving to others in some capacity. I have consistently taught my children that the gifts God has given us are for the benefit of others and not for ourselves. After all, the apple is not for the apple tree; it is for us.

My vision to live this outrageous, crazy dream has beautifully manifested itself into my reality. I believe our dreams are given to us in pictures first, and we must plant the seeds of belief daily until we see them come into full fruition. Consider this: Let's say you have a pack of wildflower seeds and you can see on the package how beautiful they will look if you plant them and tend them. If you can believe in a photo on a pack of seeds, why can't you believe the picture in your mind of you succeeding WILDLY?

It is true that whatever we believe, we can achieve; so it is critical to plant your seeds with absolute faith, despite how it looks in the beginning.

The seeds I have been planting daily for the past 24 years will yield fruit for many years to come, because that is how dreams work. If God is to be the author of our dreams, whatever we pursue will impact those around us in a positive way. Even after we are gone, those seeds will continue to sow life into others.

My questions to you are this: "What are you planting and how determined are you to achieve your dream?"

I feel that I'm only at the dawn of my life, and I believe my dreams are just beginning to break out in a way that will inspire those around me. I bet you are saying to yourself right now, if Jamie can achieve her "crazy" dream, then I can too! That is EXACTLY the purpose for this book.

What were the odds of this abandoned, broken, single mom achieving her dream? The world said it was a LONG SHOT, but what does the world know anyway? It was God who gave me the dream and I was brave enough to work toward making it reality. I dare you to break free from your cocoon, say good-bye to your crawling caterpillar, and take flight into your brave beginning.

CHAPTER 2

Believe to Achieve

Bob Williamson

We're addressing the need to believe in yourself and your dreams early in the book because it is essential to have that faith. If you doubt your abilities and think you'll probably fail, it is highly likely you will.

You have to believe in order to achieve. This is an axiom you should memorize.

I don't claim to have all the answers for teaching you how to be successful, but I do have a fascinating life story with such a bizarre and amazing transformation that it warrants an objective look at my methodology. The obvious conclusion is that if it worked for someone like me, it will definitely work for you.

I frequently speak in prisons, rehabilitation centers, and rescue missions to those who've lost belief in themselves and given up hope. One of the saddest things I ever saw was at Mercy Ministries in Nashville, Tennessee. I had been invited to give a motivational talk to the young women there. In the lobby was a large cross covered in Post-it Notes, and on the notes the young ladies had written opinions of themselves. Tears welled up in my eyes as I read them: "I'm worthless." "I'm scum." "I'm bad." "I'm no good." "Whore." "Sick." "I'm stupid." I didn't see one positive statement.

The women seeking shelter there had been sexually, mentally, and physically abused for most of their young lives, but curiously blamed themselves. The ministry's founder, Nancy Alcorn, explained that one of the most difficult problems she faces in trying to rehabilitate these youngsters is convincing them that their abusers are the ones who are sick, no good, and bad. They are innocent victims and have no reason to feel guilt.

I remember running away from home when I was a boy, riding my bicycle far into the countryside where I sat on a hill with tears streaming down my face, staring into the distance, wondering why I was so worthless and why my father constantly called me stupid and said I'd never amount to anything. It may sound bizarre, but I sometimes fight those feelings even today. It is amazing how our childhood can impact our future if we dwell on it and allow it to direct us.

I told the girls at Mercy to envision riding in an automobile and looking out of the large front windshield. The rearview mirror is tiny in comparison, and accordingly we don't spend much time looking in it at what's behind us as we drive. Instead we gaze at all of the new things unfolding ahead of us. That's how life should be. When I look in the rearview mirror of my life, I don't like what I see. So I try my utmost to look forward and focus on each new day as a fascinating opportunity to positively impact the world.

I have nothing to gain from you adopting my plan aside from the satisfaction of extending a helping hand. I urge you to keep an open mind and give this faith-based, life-changing system a chance.

The Bible has been my step-by-step guide for

redemption and for personal and business success. It's full of advice on any subject, and its Author is no ordinary writer; He is Almighty God. I've read the Bible cover to cover countless times. I begin each day by studying it and searching for the answers I need to guide me—and I always find them.

Essential to believing in yourself is understanding that God doesn't view you as you currently are, but rather as what you can be through His help and guidance. The world looked at me and saw a long-haired, dirty-hippie drug addict; a criminal full of hate, bitterness, and rage But Almighty God saw me as I am today and where I will be in 10 million years.

It Becomes Possible When You Stop Believing It's Impossible.

Yes! You can succeed in ways that you and everyone else never considered remotely possible for someone with your perceived "qualifications." I fulfilled my dreams by first believing in myself, despite what others thought.

The experts thought the world was flat, and Christopher Columbus proved them wrong. They said Earth was the center of the universe, and Galileo deflated that one. They said flying faster than the speed of sound was impossible, but Chuck Yeager showed otherwise. "Experts" said for years that the human body was incapable of running a sub-four-minute mile, and *you were crazy to even try it.* But Roger Bannister did it in 1954. And once he did it, everyone was doing it. Today high-schoolers routinely run faster than a four-minute mile, and in the past 50 years the record has been lowered by almost *17 seconds.* All of which underlines an important lesson: *Once you stop believing something is impossible, it becomes possible.*

All these pseudo-intellectual naysayers had one thing in common; they were quite certain their hypotheses were correct, right up until the moment their theories exploded in their faces.

The problem with "experts" is that s-o-o-o many people believe them.

Bobby Bowden, of Florida State University, is the second-winningest coach in the history of collegiate football. He went through a rough period, feeling he was one great player away from success. He said it was irrelevant whether it was a quarterback, tight end, or linebacker; he just needed one inspiring player *who believed he could win every game* and was willing to go all out to do so. That type of attitude is empowering and infectious, not only by setting up individual great plays, but also motivating and inspiring others on the team to believe that they will win and to give it their all. Bowden says it's the difference between being good and great, being an also-ran and winning championships.

As a CEO, I most value employees who exhibit the attributes of a cheerful, optimistic, winning attitude. Believing that something can be accomplished is vital. If you do not believe, trust me, you have virtually no chance of achieving it. This is true for all genders, ethnicities, and, yes, even ages.

Colonel Harland Sanders was an entrepreneur who didn't become a professional chef until he was 40, didn't franchise Kentucky Fried Chicken until he was 62, and didn't become an icon until after he sold his multibillion-dollar company at 75. In fact, at age 65 Colonel Sanders was still living on his monthly $105 Social Security check. But he possessed a very tasty secret recipe for fried chicken that was "finger-lickin' good" *and* a belief that people would love it. For years, he carried the secret formula in his head and the spice mixture in his car.

Colonel Sanders didn't let his age slow him down. He acted as though his birth certificate was wrong. He launched his second career by driving across the country, cooking batches of fried chicken for restaurant owners and their employees. If the reaction was favorable, he entered into a handshake agreement that stipulated he'd be paid a nickel for each chicken sold. By 1964, he had more than 600 franchised outlets in North America.

As a fellow entrepreneur, I know what it takes to build a business from the ground up with no start-up capital, and I admire such energy, perseverance, patience, and stamina. The wonderful optimistic "can-do" attitude that he exhibited is something to behold. He believed in himself and his product, and it turned out to be a winning combination.

Stories like his (and ours) clearly demonstrate that wherever you are in life, *anyone* can achieve success. It is not reserved for a chosen few. So start believing in yourself and your ideas *today*.

CHAPTER 2

Believe to Achieve

Jamie Vrinios

The greatest stories ever told involve a brave individual daring to go first and bust through the belief barriers the herd proclaimed "impossible." Bob and I are two examples of countless people who have done that. But everyone has been created with unique gifts specifically designed to contribute to others in a positive way. The key is recognizing them.

The Bible teaches us to *"stir up the gift of God which is in you"* (2 Timothy 1:6), and that's pretty exciting. God has destined and purposed us to WIN within our gifting and to celebrate one another. When we embrace this truth it releases us into extraordinary possibilities. When we operate within our gifting we win by divine design, but when we try to be someone we're not, we lose.

If you want to WIN you must SEE IT first, just like that package of wildflower seeds I mentioned in Chapter 1. If you want the vision in your mind and heart to manifest into reality, write it down and encourage yourself in it daily. If you really believe in your dreams you can't help but pursue them relentlessly and unapologetically. You'll be driven by a deep-down "knowing" that this is what you were created for.

There is a difference between believing and mentally agreeing. I have worked with countless leaders who say they believe, but their inaction proves otherwise. If you believe in the picture of wildflowers, that the seeds will grow into a beautiful garden, then plant them in the ground with faith. You are a walking package of seeds, my friend, so start sowing with BELIEF.

A leader who only mentally agrees tends to give up when the transformation begins. Some people may believe just enough to plant the seeds in the ground, but their belief is not strong enough to nurse the seedlings through the storms. The storms always reveal our belief, and it is in the moments of pressure that we must decide to keep moving. It's a YES or NO moment. Do you move forward through the metamorphosis into a new beginning, or do you just exist in the cage of the status quo? I believe if you are brave enough to answer YES, you will exceed beyond anything you ever dreamed possible.

The daily discipline that's required to succeed will ignite your faith and fan the flame inside your heart to never give up. When vision is lacking, so is confidence. You will only enjoy outrageous success when your vision becomes your obsession. Dreams will come to fruition when you make excellence a part of the process. I believe God's design for us is excellence, and that is why our vision is a beautiful reminder to invite Him along in our pursuit of it.

You can rise up with God-confidence or self-confidence, and they are two very different mind-sets. Self-confidence is believing you can make it on just your own effort, that if you work long and hard enough you will meet the mark. God-confidence is believing that if you work diligently you will reach your goal, but there's an additional peace in knowing the fight is fixed in your favor. God-confidence means that no matter what adversity comes your way, you'll remain steady because deep down you know the ending: YOU WIN!

The preview of your finish, just like that picture of flowers, was already played out in your mind at the beginning of the journey. Miracles happen where there is great expectation and belief. If you fear failure, you will never take the risks required to experience great victory.

Tolerance or intolerance of our present determines our future. If as a baby you had refused to walk because you feared falling, where would you be today? Even as a child you knew you had to fall in order to rise. Apply this to your current state of mind; maybe you are still crawling and never knew it until you picked up this book. To WIN you must SEE yourself at the BEGINNING of the race already a CHAMPION.

Let me ask you a question: If you knew you couldn't fail, what would you dare to believe? The dreamer who believes with zero doubt manifests radical results. The evidence of belief is action, and this requires that you have the guts and grit to never back up, even if you have to forge ahead solo.

Have you ever been inspired by anyone who achieved the impossible with *no* obstacles? Of course not! If you were to take a poll of everyone who achieved greatness, I bet they all persevered through adversity.

Let me ask you another question: When you encounter obstacles and it seems impossible to hit the mark, what is the number one ingredient that guarantees you'll stay in the race and finish? It's BELIEF. After 24 years of developing leaders and coaching them to their goals, I have found it is their

BELIEF that guarantees the win. That's the mind-set that drives them to get back up over and over again. If you want to succeed in life, your mind must be SET to never give up.

"Your beliefs become your thoughts, your thoughts become your actions, your actions become your habits, your habits become your values, your values become your destiny." – Gandhi

"So you see faith by itself isn't enough, unless it produces good deeds, it is dead and useless" – (James 2:17).

I love stories of "firsts," of people who pave the way for those who have allowed disbelief to get in their way. It's amazing how one person who believes enough to take action can be a catalyst for the masses. All champions understand that when they make their dreams come true, they open the floodgates of belief for others.

One of my favorite stories (that exemplifies this kind of mind-set) involves Olympic gymnast Kerri Strug. In 1996 she was the U.S. team's golden child and a sure bet to win gold at the Atlanta Games. But when she landed after her first vault, she fell and heard something snap in her foot. She lost all sensation in her leg.

WOW, so everyone is counting on her but she can't even feel her leg. Can you imagine? It was her YES or NO moment, huh? Kerri's coach encouraged her to try to get through one more run, and that is what the 18-year-old did. Kerri landed the vault for a 9.712, and the U.S. team won its FIRST Olympic championship in this event.

Kerri had a champion's mind-set with the kind of belief that is required to realize dreams. After the ceremony, doctors found two torn ligaments in her ankle. It was a miracle she could even walk let alone run and FLY over that vault to pull off a victory that made history.

If you want to succeed, you must be willing to work through pain. And you must believe like a champion believes and operate from God-confidence. This creates the environment for the miraculous. So never doubt the destination, but at the same time be sure to enjoy the journey. The process is just as important as what it produces.

Here's a lesson from author Paulo Coelho that I love: "A man spent hours watching a butterfly struggling to emerge out of its cocoon. It managed to make a tiny hole but its body was too large to get through it. After a long struggle, it appeared to be exhausted and remained absolutely still. The man decided to help the butterfly and with a pair of scissors, he cut open the cocoon, thus releasing it. However, the butterfly's body was very small and wrinkled and its wings were crumpled. The man continued to watch hoping that at any moment, it would open its wings and fly away. Nothing happened, in fact, the butterfly spent the rest of its brief life dragging around its shrunken body and shriveled wings, incapable of flight."

"What the man, (out of kindness and eagerness to help), had failed to understand was the tight cocoon and the efforts the butterfly had to make to squeeze out of that tiny hole was nature's way of training the butterfly and of strengthening its wings.

Sometimes, a little extra effort is precisely what prepares us for the next obstacle to be faced. Anyone who refuses to make that effort, or gets the wrong sort of help, is left unprepared to fight the next battle and never manages to fly off to their destiny."

So focus on the finish, never the fight. Your bravest moment is when you choose to stop crawling and take flight.

CHAPTER 3

The Power of Passion

Bob Williamson

In addition to building confidence in yourself and believing you can succeed, unbridled *passion* is a vital consideration for increasing the odds for success in your undertaking. There is power in passion and you need to tap into it.

Passion is essential for achieving success. In simple terms it means you love what you are doing. Work is not work when you are passionate about your mission; you will never dread going to work or hope for Friday to hurry up and arrive. Actually, true passion ensures that when working extra hours becomes necessary, as it sometimes will, you will *desire* to work them.

You might be shaking your head in wonderment at such a statement, but if you are passionate about what you do, you will be having fun and doing something you love. Those of us who are passionate about what we do are referred to as 24/7 people, because we are consumed by our passions, and our "work" is always with us.

For sure it's not all fun and games to tackle a major mission and work toward its accomplishment, but passionate people are driven by an innate, unquenchable craving to excel. We will tenaciously fight through the obstacles and storms of life in order to feed our passions. Mine is so intense that it reminds me of crawling across a blazing-hot desert for days on end without water. The insatiable thirst pushing my poor soul to find water before it's too late is akin to my dramatic passion and desire to succeed at whatever I'm undertaking. It is the fuel that feeds the very depths of my soul and unquestionably is a driving force behind any success I've enjoyed.

I've founded 19 different companies, a church, and a global ministry and have been passionate about every one of them. My first and favorite companies all had something to do with wildlife and the great outdoors. I've loved hunting, fishing, and being afield at every opportunity for most of my life, and I even became a wildlife artist as a hobby so I could enjoy my passion even when I was at home. I enjoyed it so much that nearly every night I was in my basement studio working far into the night to create my wildlife art renderings. And to be sure, at most every opportunity including holidays and weekends, I was afield enjoying all of God's creatures and the outdoor wonderland that He so masterfully created.

Imagine how awesome it was to earn a living doing something I absolutely loved. To be a wildlife artist was equivalent to *"living the dream."* I've heard airline pilots tell me of their love of flying and how bizarre it seemed that someone would actually pay them to do something that they loved. I share that sentiment, and with every company I founded I liked what I was doing.

I urge you to do likewise with your passions.

With that said, a word of caution is in order here: Just because you enjoy something doesn't mean you should do it for a living. There are practical considerations that must be carefully weighed. You might enjoy and have unbridled passion for flying kites, but it might prove very difficult to make a living at it.

Most everyone has heard the expression *"starving artist."* I found out rather quickly that there was a reason for that saying, and it is founded upon the axiom that many artists barely survive financially through their art. Though I was exceedingly passionate about my painting, my love for it extraordinary, and my skill as an artist above average, it didn't take me long to realize I was not good enough or patient enough to create the masterpieces that commanded the serious money. Besides, even if I could have made a living from my art, I was not connected to a "dream maker" in that field who could introduce me to those big-bucks buyers who can make someone's career.

Shortly after I went into business as a wildlife artist, I quickly discovered (the hard way) that merely being passionate about what one does will not pay the bills. Shortly after I established my wildlife art studio, I found myself facing mounting bills and scrambling to find money to pay them. Up until the point I went into business for myself I'd made decent money as a plant manager at a paint company. That income combined with the profits from selling my wildlife art on the side and my wife's compensation from her job meant we'd been doing very well, and we had a nice home with a swimming pool. But like most families we would spend right up to the limits of our income and had no savings. My start-up capital for my first business consisted of $1,000 that I borrowed on my credit card, and it was a tenuous situation.

Ugh! This scenario did not fit well with two of my other passions: the first being that I wanted to become a multimillionaire. I'd spent years homeless, starving on the streets, and struggling just to survive. Unlike many people I was confident that I could become a multimillionaire and didn't think it was out of reach for me. I felt there was nothing all that special about the people who'd achieved it, and I felt sure they put their pants on the same way I do every morning. I suppose in retrospect my attitude was a tad arrogant and overconfident; however, one thing is sure in life and business, if you don't *believe* it, you cannot *achieve* it.

My second passion was in line with the first. I was passionate about proving those folks wrong who had told me things such as: I would never succeed. I was a "bad seed," and a loser. I shouldn't have cared about what they thought or wasted time thinking about them, but I was passionate about showing they were wrong and making a statement. It was highly motivational, especially when I faltered and the thought of quitting flashed across my mind. I just couldn't bear the thought of hearing them say "I told you so," and would redouble my efforts to continue onward.

After surviving what I'd been through, I was convinced that working smart and hard would make up for my lack of formal education and experience. I had faith that with God's help I could do it, but I knew my art renderings weren't going to make it happen. Fortunately, I realized that being passionate about something isn't limited to a single-faceted endeavor, nor impractical, and I could realize all my dreams by being flexible. So I found a way to stay in a field I absolutely loved, wildlife art, and make millions of dollars, and show those naysayers they were wrong about me. The plan I came up with enabled me to fulfill all three of my passions.

My strategy was to supplement my income from being a wildlife artist by selling products, supplies, and services to other artists. I developed a paint system for them that was so good that it was hailed as a technological breakthrough and remains the number one airbrush paint in the industry to this very day. Then I expanded to other areas and added over 5,000 artist supplies and products (many that I invented). I built a manufacturing plant to produce scores of my products, including paint, dry chemicals used by artists, clays and papier-mâché, and a urethane-injection molding operation. I founded numerous world-renowned outdoors and wildlife art shows and competitions, and I wrote how-to books, created videos, and founded the leading magazine for wildlife artists. Soon I had 286,000 customers and seven distributers worldwide, and the dollars were pouring in.

I looked for and found a career that I was passionate about and enjoyed immensely. At the same time, I could make enough money to fulfill my dream of becoming a multimillionaire and simultaneously prove to those naysayers who ridiculed me that I wasn't just a worthless bum. I also proved to myself once and for all there was no longer any need to have such low self-esteem.

It took passion, believing in myself, vision, working long

hours, sacrifice, perseverance, great employees, and working smart, but I would be remiss if I left out my greatest asset, my tremendous faith in my God who was the source of my passion and self-confidence and was right there with me through the worst and best of times.

CHAPTER 3

The Power of Passion

Jamie Vrinios

One of my favorite quotes is by Mark Twain: "The two most important days in your life are the day you are born and the day you find out why." An individual who has identified their "why" instinctively has the passion to unapologetically pursue their goals and dreams. Vision and passion go together like heat and fire. Passion is the spark and is defined as an intense desire or enthusiasm toward something. Its opposite is apathy and indifference.

As I think back on my poverty years, I realize I was confronted with yes or no moments. In these times, my passion and purpose became crystal clear. (If you want to succeed in life, they must.) Believe me, I legitimately had some great excuses to give up, but instead I was passionate about providing my children and myself a bright future, and that drove me again and again to get back up from every knockdown.

It doesn't matter what circumstances you face. When you have passion, it summons you to rise up and fight for what you believe in. Every single one of us is faced with our yes or no moments, and it is in that moment that we decide to overcome the challenges thrown our way or choose to lie down and quit. I believe the greatest of teachers have walked through the darkest of valleys, and it is there that someone truly discovers their "fire." Will an individual have what it takes to come out of adversity with more fire and passion than ever? Many refer to that ability as our "calling," "purpose," "destiny," and many more adjectives. But the truth in simple terms is: *It is just a deep-down burning fire that you can't ignore.* It's a determination that sets you apart and pushes you to move without hesitation toward your dreams. Passion is the grit and guts rolled into one that will guarantee you'll cross that finish line.

> *"He who knows and knows that he knows is a wise man—follow him; he who knows not and knows not that he knows not is a fool—shun him."*
> – Confucius

An individual who hesitates just doesn't "know," and someone who moves passionately with zero doubt toward a dream just knows, and that "knowing" is "fire." It is impossible for mankind to remove the flame that God has put inside of us. It is what we have been created to live out, so in simple terms, you are just straight up "BORN FOR THIS." The "flame" is in you, and the only thing you must do is stay in the race and be determined to finish well. There will be those who will magnify the flame inside your heart and many more who will try to put your fire out, but they can't compete with our Creator who put it there from the beginning, before you were born.

I was fortunate to find this "fire" early on in my life. Without it, my life would have ended up very differently. I want you to imagine for just one moment an entire family turning its back on my children and me and for a lifetime. How did I overcome it?

"FIRE"

I just knew deep down in my spirit that I was born for something greater, something that was awaiting me on just the other side of my pain. You see, God isn't looking for someone who has it "all together." He is a master at taking our pain and turning it into something beautiful, and He delights in doing so.

"But God chose the foolish things of the world to shame the wise. God chose the weak things of the world to shame the strong" – (1 Corinthians 1:27).

You must be passionate about living out your destiny unapologetically, and where the "fire" resides, the commitment to never give up is a given. You will never have to be "convinced" of your dream—it's this fire that keeps you "lit up," "fired up," and willing to "RISE up" under any circumstance.

When you have genuinely made a commitment to make your move toward your dreams, there is no plan B. You must enter the arena of life seeing yourself as a WINNER and refusing to play small.

"There is no passion to be found playing small— in settling for a life that is less than the one you are capable of living." – Nelson Mandela

At a young age, I took an unyielding stance in my life to ensure that my children would never experience the pain and rejection I felt as a little girl. It was my driving force 32 years ago and remains the center of everything I pursue today.

While I may not be that scared, young, single mom living in poverty any longer, there are plenty surrounding me who are. If you look around this world, there are people everywhere who have been forgotten, abandoned, rejected, abused, misunderstood, and labeled by society as "rejects." I am absolutely addicted and unapologetic in my passionate pursuit of encouraging and helping those individuals the world has forgotten. In fact, there is nothing I love more than to see the individual who NOBODY would have bet on prove the world wrong and WIN.

These are the greatest passion stories ever told, and I find great joy in proving the so-called experts in this world wrong. I know God did not rescue me in order to offer His love exclusively to me. He stands ready to adopt all who will invite Him into their life. It gets back to the apple tree example, doesn't it? That is, the tree bears fruit for others, not for itself.

The scars in our lives are a constant reminder of just how strong we are, and we can turn those experiences into help for others or not, it's our choice. As I mentioned in the last chapter, it is the leader who goes "first" who opens the floodgates of belief for others, and this, my friend, cannot happen without passion.

Two years ago, my son, Sam, became a Florida state track and field champion in the 4x100 meter relay competition. Sam had a passion that was "on steroids" in pursuit of this goal. I will never forget how as a freshman in high school he had a coach who told him he wasn't fast enough, but the truth was this man just didn't like him. Sam made a decision to prove his coach wrong and worked tirelessly day and night running and strengthening himself in order to win. Many along the way told him he should run the quarter mile because he was better suited for this race; however, his "passion" was to run the 4x100, which meant he had to work even harder in order to become a state champion.

By the time Sam was a junior in high school his speed forced the coaches to throw away their preconceived opinions. I loved attending his meets and watching the shocked look on their faces as they watched him run. In Sammy's senior year, the 4x100 meter relay team he was on made it to the finals, and were faced with their yes or no moment of breaking a record held for over 100 years.

WOW!

The invitation for this team to go "first" in setting a new record and NEW beginning for Manatee High School 4A Division was a reality. We had dinner together the night before the race and Sammy demonstrated a deep, clear, intense passion as we spoke about him winning the next day. He said he saw the finish line in his mind and that the relay team was going to win the championship. Because of the passion he expressed that night I knew Sam had zero doubt that he would soon be celebrating victory.

You see, there was no option for Sam. You could feel it in his countenance and see it in his eyes. He had a radiant energy that exuded from him, and it was contagious. Passion is a contagion that all champions understand, and it determines whether we win or lose in sports—or life.

The next day, we went to the state finals and there were many opinions out there about which team would win. I noticed Sam off by himself staying singularly focused on the race. Even though I was hundreds of yards away I could easily see the raging passion to win firmly planted on his determined face.

The race was undoubtedly one of the most exciting days for me as a mom, cheering my son to cross the finish line and secure the win, and best of all I knew it would become a marker in Sam's life that he would never forget. Manatee High School's 4x100 team was victorious that day and became the new state champion. As the team members stood together on the platform during the award ceremony, and as the state champion medal was put around each runner's neck, the joy on their faces was indescribable. They broke a 100-year record that day and made history. All records are made to be broken, and that is exactly what they accomplished. The victory was ever so sweet.

The title of champion can never be removed from Sam, because once declared a champion you are always a champion. I believe that is one reason why having the passion to win in life is imperative to our confidence in reaching our destiny. Do you remember the coach I mentioned who, during Sam's freshman year, told him he wasn't fast enough? I just have to say thank you to this coach because his discouragement only ignited the fire and passion in Sam's heart to win. Ironically, that coach was there on that winning day when that medal was hung around my son's neck.

How bad do you want to succeed in life? If you want to see your dreams manifest themselves into reality, you must be ALL IN, singularly focused, and passionate. Sam and the three other runners demonstrated all of those qualities on that day, and they won.

What is that fire deep down inside of you that someone

has tried to put out with negativity and discouragement? I hope you are inspired to ignite those inner flames, and if knocked down let them help you rise again and again, sparked by this book. The obstacles and naysayers along the way will only increase your passion if you believe with zero doubt in your goals and understand your why.

I could encourage the champion in Sam because I've lived with this same mind-set throughout my life and have had the passion to arise even in my darkest moments to achieve my dreams. I hope you can look at all those who have said you can never do it and say thank you as you bravely pursue your dreams with unapologetic passion.

TRUTH: Every single one of us is born to win, and you will dance right over the finish line when you live with passion.

I want to emphasize that you must WANT this with all your heart and be willing to go against "herd mentality." The only ones who know what you are capable of doing are you and the God who created you and gave you the vision in the first place.

Mary Kay Ash said, "Most people live and die with their music still unplayed. They never dare to try." I hope as you turn the next page of your story that your music will inspire those around you to live with passion. I want to end my portion of this chapter with the story of "The Violin Prodigy." It is my goal as you read this to help you recognize that it is the "fire" inside of us that gives us the ability to never give up on our dreams no matter what the naysayers may say.

The Violin Prodigy Story

A young violin prodigy was walking down the street
one day, trying to decide whether or not to pursue a
life in music, when he came upon the most famous
violin teacher in the world. Scarcely believing his luck,
he stopped the great teacher and asked if he could play
for him, thinking he would abandon his dream of a
career in music if the great teacher told him he was
wasting his time.

The great teacher nodded silently for him to begin.
So he played, beads of sweat soon appearing on his
forehead, and when he finished, he was certain he'd
given his finest performance. But the great maestro
only shook his head sadly and said, "You lack the fire."

The young musician was devastated. Nevertheless,
he returned home and announced his intention to
abandon the violin. Instead, he entered the world of
business and turned out to have such a talent for it
that in a few short years he found himself richer than
he'd ever imagined possible.

Almost a decade later he found himself walking
down another street in another city when he
happened to spot the great teacher again. He rushed
over to him. "I'm so sorry to bother you," he said,
"and I'm sure you don't remember me, but I stopped
you on the street years ago to play my violin for you,
and I just want to thank you. Because of your advice,
I abandoned my greatest love, the violin, painful as it
was, and became a businessman, and today I enjoy
great success, which I owe all to you. But one thing

you must tell me: How did you know I didn't have what it takes? How did you know all those years ago I lacked the fire?"

The great teacher shook his head sadly and said only, "You don't understand. I tell everyone who plays for me they lack the fire. If you had the fire, you wouldn't have listened." – Unknown

The "fire" inside is God's gift to us, and what we choose to do with it is our gift back to Him. I can only imagine the JOY He must experience when He looks upon each of us as we dance freely in our gifts and passionately live out our God-given dreams. You are created to SHINE, so never apologize for letting your light SHINE before others; it pleases the Father, who created you.

"In the same way, let your light shine before others, that they may see your good deeds and glorify your Father in Heaven" – (Matthew 5:16).

~Do it with passion or not at all.~

BOB WILLIAMSON AND JAMIE VRINIOS

CHAPTER 4

Naysayers

Bob Williamson

Developing a vision of what you wish to accomplish can be a rewarding experience. It can also be very discouraging.

One thing you will find if you undertake anything of significance is that you will receive plenty of advice. Unfortunately, the overwhelming majority of it will be negative. My recommendation, however, is that no matter how discouraging it might seem to carefully listen to all advice, both solicited and unsolicited, analyze the situation, and then follow your heart.

I vividly remember the day I quit the last job I ever worked for anyone else. I'd grown to despise working for managers who messed up everything they touched and then tried to shift the blame to others, including me. In short I was sick and tired of taking orders from people who attained their positions through tenure or as political brownnosers. I considered them to be idiots, and my current immediate supervisor fit that description perfectly.

I liked my responsibilities just fine, but intensely disliked having to take orders from this guy. His nickname was Junior, and he was about 5-feet nothing and had a "short man" complex. He didn't have the slightest idea about how to run a paint company, but his daddy owned it. When he finally did show up for work at midmorning, he'd spend most of his time stalking around yelling at people like he was a tough guy.

He had yet to raise his voice at me and for good reason. In short order I'd transformed the paint manufacturing plant from a nightmare into a smooth-running machine. I was the first to arrive on the job and the last to leave. I worked hard and smart and did an excellent job. The first thing I did when I took over was fire nearly every employee in the plant and then replace them with employees who'd work. Within six months the programs that I'd implemented turned the little company around and nearly doubled its profit margin. With each ensuing success, I received more responsibility, and soon enough in addition to running the manufacturing plant, I was managing the warehouse, and the shipping and purchasing departments. Except for the sales and administration departments, I was running the entire company.

One day Junior called me into his office and immediately began yelling at me like I was a 4-year-old child. He hadn't checked his facts, and what he perceived to be a problem hadn't even happened.

When he raised his voice at me, it was as though he'd opened my dark side's cage door and released the black fury that'd been held in check since my life had been transformed by Jesus in Grady Hospital. It was as though it had been impatiently awaiting the opportunity to rip someone to pieces.

My mind snapped and then exploded. All the pent-up rage and frustration building in me from all the assorted jerks I'd worked for during the past few years bubbled to the surface and spewed all over him, like a Coke that had been dropped on the floor and popped open in his face. I angrily screamed, *"You little sawed off runt! That's it! I'm sick and tired of your stupidity and your big mouth. I quit! Now you either write my check this very minute or I'm gonna beat you within an inch of your life right here and right now!*

I was standing over him with both fists clenched, and if he even blinked I was prepared to bash his head in. I was breathing like a raging bull and just as wild-eyed. Several office workers were present, but they sat with eyes lowered, too afraid to breathe much less offer assistance to Junior. No one moved, looked up, or said a word.

With a shaking hand and a scared look on his face, he wrote my final paycheck. As I drove home I was still mad as a wasp knocked off its nest. I was sick and tired of working for others. Suddenly I banged my fist on the dashboard of the car and shouted, *"I'll never work for anyone else again!"* And I haven't!

And with that bold statement my entrepreneurial career was born.

As I look back on that decision today, I realize that it was reckless, rash, impulsive, irresponsible, naive, and more correctly, just outright stupid. I had no start-up capital except for the check he had just written me, no formal education in business management, no research of revenue potential, no analysis of the competitive landscape, and I didn't have a business plan. For that matter I didn't even know what type of business I wanted to start.

So, as word got around my personal network that I'd quit my job and I was going to start my own business, the naysayers came out of their nests in droves. True to form, my dad told me that it was one of the stupidest things that I'd ever done and, incredibly, wanted me to go back and apologize to my former employer and see if I could get my job back. My brother followed suite by telling me that I was a moron. My wife was so livid that she wouldn't even speak to me. Her dad, my friends and neighbors, and essentially everyone that I knew told me that it was insanity to even think of giving up my high-paying job to start my own business.

The only exception was my wife's mother, Jenny. One Sunday afternoon shortly after I'd quit my job, the entire family was assembled in my in-laws' backyard for a cookout. They were all sitting around berating me about quitting and telling me how many new businesses fail and how I needed to get a "regular job."

Jenny listened to them beating me up and then got fighting mad and angrily bellowed out to them in a stern voice, *"Listen, if Bob Williamson says he's going to make it, then he's going to make it, clear and simple! That's all there is to it. Now LEAVE HIM ALONE!"*

I loved Jenny with all my heart for expressing such confidence in me that day. She was the only person that I can ever remember who showed me any respect or exuded confidence in my ability to succeed. Her unwavering faith in me meant more than anyone could imagine, and it's something that I'll continue to cherish until the day I die. I loved her like I loved my own mother.

Someone could've pulled my fingernails out and I still wouldn't have admitted that I was hurt by everyone's lack of confidence in me, but deep down I was very hurt by it. The only positive thing about their lack of faith in me was that it was motivating. I became steadfastly resolved to wipe those smirks off their faces and show every one of them that they were wrong about me (and in just a few months I did just that).

Naysayers aren't content just to discourage others from attempting to attain a dream, and if you ignore their negativity and go forward anyway, they will try to get you to quit at every opportunity (especially if you stumble). Every business has its ups and downs. It seems that when things are going the worst and you are down and discouraged, it triggers these cynics to attack with a vengeance.

As an example, one time several years after I had started my companies, 13 of my trusted employees embezzled nearly $1 million from my very profitable and successful business WASCO. It was a serious situation. They had started a company identical to mine to directly compete with me, and had stolen everything they could get their hands on and destroyed all my financial records in the process. The events that followed were nightmarish. When I discovered through my insurance agent that the ringleader (my comptroller) was planning to start his own business, identical to mine, I immediately fired him. The next day a dozen of my high- and low-level employees quit with no notice and went to work for his new company, which he began running out of his home basement.

When I tried to examine my accounting records, I discovered that my general ledger had been erased and all company backup tapes were missing. Computer records were not the only thing missing; hard-copy files were missing too. All my vendor files were empty, and I had no way of knowing how much or to whom money might be owed. The same held true for receivables and taxes; even our bank reconcilements were nowhere to be found. All my accounting data had disappeared! My comptroller had been very busy.

I hastily ordered a physical inventory to be conducted and made the sickening discovery that approximately $300,000 of inventory was missing. That translated to 80 percent of my inventory; in effect my shelves were bare.

Next we checked with the bank and discovered that my bank account was empty. It got worse. Because there were no funds, I was bouncing checks like crazy. (WASCO had never bounced a check.) When we reached overdrawn status, the bank honored the checks for a while, but soon that courtesy was cut off and checks were being returned. An unbelievable $275,000 in bad checks had amassed.

When I heard this piece of news I remembered my comptroller working all those late nights and bringing me hundreds of checks to sign, along with a report showing that I would still have $25,000 available after signing them and bringing payables completely current. In reality he had stolen me blind.

I soon discovered that everyone with whom I had any financial dealings dropped me like a hot rock. At the first sign of trouble my so-called friends scattered like cockroaches when a light was turned on. Sadly, I found out that most were friends when the money was flowing and I was riding high, but after the fall it was "See ya later." My entourage and supporters were gone as soon as the money disappeared. The mover-and-shaker club members around town who had constantly come at my office courting me were among the first to go, beginning with my banker, who was threatening to sue.

My suppliers were next. The bank had closed my account when the checks started hitting, and as soon as it quit covering any of those payments nearly 300 of my vendors received NSF checks that could not be sent back through the bank again. All my "good friends" throughout the industry were refusing to provide me with credit or even ship to me until I made good on those checks. Many were threatening to take me to court.

In just three days I discovered that I had no inventory, no money to buy more, no friends, no credit extension from my suppliers. And no one in their right mind was going to loan me money with my financial records in ruin.

With no inventory or funds to buy more, I couldn't ship orders and earn money, nor could I make payroll, pay utilities, UPS, or pay anything. The situation was critical and I had no choice but to immediately order a massive layoff. I reduced our workforce from 65 employees to just 19 in three days. I completely closed our plant in Idaho, and all those employees lost their jobs.

I called the remaining employees together and briefed them on what I knew so far. I provided excruciating detail about the theft, and I was honest in telling them that the situation was grim and I wasn't sure if we could even recover from what appeared to be a massive theft of most of our current assets. I told them our business cash and inventory were gone and that we'd been deliberately sabotaged. Our financial records had been destroyed and lies had been spread all over town about me.

I warned that as we fought our way through this situation that there were no guarantees I would be capable of paying them on time and if they remained on board, issuing paychecks could be sporadic and entirely dependent upon cash receipts.

The situation was ugly and they needed to know. These were the most loyal of the loyal employees that I had, and as I looked around the room I could see the concern on their faces. They loved the company, but they had bills to pay and mortgage obligations. I wouldn't blame them if they resigned.

If God's goal was to humble me, He succeeded. I didn't feel arrogant anymore, and I definitely didn't feel much like the marketing-genius boy wonder I'd convinced myself I was. Helplessly I looked around at what had once been the mighty WASCO machine. I thought of all the hard work, planning, and awesome results. It was all I could do to keep from crying.

In the days that ensued, every expert I turned to for advice on my crisis, including my insurance agent, attorney, and banker, all advised me that it would be impossible to avoid bankruptcy and that I might as well just get on with it.

The party was over!

Shortly after that, my CPA, called and asked for a meeting (and invited himself to dinner). He suggested that we could talk while we fished and afterward my wife could fry up our catch and we could continue our discussion over dinner. I welcomed the idea; fishing would be a good diversion from the crushing pressure that I was feeling.

He came over later that afternoon and we went out on

the dock that overlooked the 2-acre pond in my backyard. We baited up our hooks with crickets and started fishing for the hungry bluegill and channel catfish that were abundantly milling around the surface, eating the handful of fish food I'd thrown in to attract them. It was a beautiful day with hardly a cloud in the deep blue sky. A casual observer watching us in that peaceful and serene setting would never have guessed the utter ruin, devastation, and chaos that I was facing.

My CPA was a very capable guy and always jovial and in a good mood. He fit the stereotype of an accountant by appearing to be somewhat of a nerd with his thick glasses, pudgy appearance, and partially balding head. He was a smart man and had been doing my taxes and advising me for five or six years, and I respected his opinion on most matters of finance.

I could tell he was greatly distressed and something was on his mind. It seemed completely out of character for him to have such a dead-serious look on his face. Finally, he seemed to muster enough courage to get whatever was bothering him off his chest. He said in his most solemn voice, "Bob, I'm your friend, and what I'm going to tell you is from one friend to another. You are an incredibly smart guy and you made a good run at this, but it's time to give it up. I've analyzed it from every angle and WASCO is just too far gone for you to salvage. You can easily get a job making good money and without question will excel at whatever you do. I'm advising you to do just that. You really shouldn't be in business for yourself."

He was no different from the rest of them. Everyone was

advising me to declare bankruptcy and call it a day. I don't know why I kept stubbornly refusing to heed their advice, but I'd taken the position that we were still a great company with a stellar reputation for the highest-quality products in the industry and outstanding customer service. As long as no one sued us, I was determined not to quit and instead rebuild WASCO to its former glory. My CPA started to reinforce his point, but I just held up my hand and sternly said,

"Shut up and fish!"

That was the last time he ever suggested that I quit.

All my life I'd been told that I couldn't or wouldn't succeed, and this turn of events made me even more determined than ever to prove them wrong. My situation was a deep hole, however, and maybe even a bottomless pit, but I was head strong—if I went down, I would go down swinging.

Ironically it had taken exactly seven years to build WASCO, and it took seven years to fight my way out of that mess. In the end, the company was doing better than it ever had, with increased revenue and double the profitability. I repaid every penny of the money that was owed and turned it into a blue-ribbon company once again.

The same is true for my other 19 companies; all were successful and I ended up financially set for life and did far better than every last one of the naysayers.

In the final analysis, most of us are far better off to ignore the naysayers and follow our dreams, and our hearts.

CHAPTER 4

Naysayers

Jamie Vrinios

Oh, how we must learn to ignore the naysayers; those negative individuals, cynics, defeatists, killjoys, and complainers who throw cold water on every idea. Merriam-Webster's dictionary defines naysayers as those individuals who say something will not work, or that it's not possible.

Hmmm.

I find great JOY in proving these negative voices wrong, and so does every brave dreamer who has ever made the wise decision to reject their "expert" opinions. The question that begs to be answered is: What makes the naysayer an expert on YOUR DREAMS? You are the one to whom God gave the vision, right?

The person who says it cannot be done should not interrupt the person who is doing it. – Chinese Proverb

Truth is, there are two types of people walking around, and they come from polar-opposite directions. The one who is an "optimist" is always looking at the positive side of life, and then we have the "pessimist," who will critically declare everything that could go wrong with any new idea or goal.

You must be forewarned and forearmed that the naysayer will always look at a situation through a pessimistic lens, so unless you want a wet blanket thrown over your "fire," my advice is to run away from these people as fast as you can. The doom and gloom individual is akin to a parasite sucking life out of your dreams.

We will always have those cynics who reject the dreamer; however, be assured there are those who will celebrate you, so go where you are celebrated and not rejected. When your mind is made up and your mission is CLEAR, you enable the "fire" inside you to SHINE ever so brightly, and without apology. The last thing you need is to share your dream with naysayers who oppose it (and pretty much everything else).

Keep in mind that this battle is waged within the mind, and as you move toward your dreams I encourage you to FIGHT with determination. The cynics will never "get it," so don't waste your time trying to convince them of something they can't even wrap their negative minds around. If you are CLEAR about your goals and sincerely BELIEVE in your vision, it becomes easy to ignore the "defeatist" and eventually it becomes second nature to you.

The true champions will always inspire the world because they refuse to allow the naysayers to distract them from courageously being the FIRST to take that road that FEW have ever DARED to travel.

If you want to WIN in life you must override any thoughts that derail you from your goals. I've always believed in getting wise counsel, and this practice has helped me tremendously over my lifetime. And there's one thing I always do before I reach out to someone for advice; I ask myself this question, "Do I respect this person in all areas of life and would I switch places with them?"

It has been my experience that finding those individuals who can speak from a place of victory and experience is rare; however, when I find these dreamers who have excelled in life, their advice and encouragement have been the wind beneath my wings.

I firmly believe that God places people in our lives to encourage us along the way. So stay connected with those who speak LIFE into your dreams. These individuals are a gift. No doubt we will also encounter those along our journey who are pessimistic. You will recognize the enthusiastic optimists because they will *fan the flame* in your heart and you will be energized when you are in their space. The pessimists will speak "doubt" into your life and dreams. If you choose to listen to them long enough their negative energy will be a slow kill to you as you move toward your destiny.

I'm sure you may think I'm making radical statements, and you would be correct in that assumption, because it will require a *radical mind-set* for you to reach your dreams.

I am reminded that with every FIRST step I ever dared to take toward accomplishing my goals I encountered those wonderful killjoy characters along the way. And you know what, they only fueled my fire and solidified my vision. This is a winning attitude. You must decide from the beginning that no matter what might happen, your mind-set must remain UNSHAKEABLE.

I vividly remember that when I announced my move to Chicago, the small-minded naysayers warned me of all the awful things that happen in the big city. The typical statement went something like: "You'll be back, Jamie, because there is no way you can ever afford to live in Chicago for very long." I was determined to prove them wrong, and I did. And you must do likewise.

COUNTLESS people made fun of me when I started my business in direct sales and entered into commission earnings versus what society labels as the "secure" paycheck. How could I step away from what the majority was saying and DARE TO DREAM? I was rejecting the "lemming mentality" of average thinking, so I became a magnet for the naysayer.

Trust me, doom and gloom individuals get uncomfortable when they see the dreamer break free from their cage, because it forces them to look inside themselves and ask tough questions. Hopefully when you are standing in the "Winner's Circle," the naysayers who attempted to drag you down to their level will be so inspired that they will choose to stop crawling and be lifted up.

When I made the decision to go into direct sales I was willing to do whatever was necessary, including eating macaroni and cheese for six months. I went into my brave beginning with a picture in my mind that was clear, bright, and UNSHAKEABLE. I was willing to do whatever it took to break free of my corporate cage, and that is exactly what I did.

You must IGNORE THE NOISE of the naysayers when you take a risk and dare to follow your dream. I was willing to sacrifice financially for the short-term so I could live a lifetime with a freedom that only an entrepreneur can enjoy. The countless number of doubters and naysayers warning me that I was going to lose money were trying to advise me about something they knew absolutely nothing about. That is why you should take counsel from those who have done it and WON. I wasn't going to line up all the quitters in direct sales and ask them "What do you think?" I went to the WINNERS and asked them their advice and followed it "to a T." I was told that my children would suffer and that I was a horrible mom, yet today if you asked my adult children about my success I know they would tell you how grateful they are that I proved all the naysayers wrong.

In fact, recently my daughter wrote me the most beautiful message that seems perfect for this chapter, and I wanted to share it here:

"Mom, I am so incredibly grateful for you. I really have been able to be a strong woman because of you. Every day I see actions I take and I'm like WOW, I'm confident enough to do that because of you, Mom. Thank you for not being a victim of your circumstances and for taking the high road. Thank you for not allowing negative people or situations to keep you from greatness, and thank you for being a good loving mom. That is a HUGE deal. I am able to get through so much more because of your perspective on life and taking any situation and making the best of it. Thank you so much. I love you immensely and cannot thank you enough for giving it your all. To go against the odds, believe in yourself, take risks, work hard, and have faith. Not a day goes by where I do not count it a blessing to be your daughter. I love you, Amber".

If you have not already, one day you will see the fruit of your efforts too. It just takes time, but it is imperative that you keep a sound mind-set and tune into the "voice of truth" in regards to your dreams.

You must be determined enough to develop this same outlook to succeed. If you want to win you must be a thermostat never a thermometer.

I work with countless leaders who have so many beautiful dreams and yet, because they are not *set* on their goal, I mean REALLY *set*, the naysayers and obstacles in their life easily derail them. For instance, many of them will make a decision to quit their job to pursue direct sales full time, and they are *so* EXCITED until they meet those fatalistic individuals who declare all the things that could go wrong instead of what is going to go right. These so-called experts who've never even DARED to dream are passing out advice to those who are willing to enter the arena. WOW! In many cases I've seen people give up before they even BEGIN. It is so sad that they listen to people who know NOTHING in regard to creating a successful life or business. If you want to WIN and LIVE out your dreams, your mind must be firmly set.

If *72 degrees Fahrenheit* is your setting, then you must stay at 72 even when adversity comes and LIFE happens, which it will. You might have people who you thought were your friends not supporting your goals. So what? You must remain set on 72. If people quit on you, money gets tight along the way, your family doesn't support you, people laugh at you, walk out on you, betray you, you must always stay at 72 in order to win.

I observe many people fluctuating when it comes to their encounters with naysayers in their life, and I believe they give these individuals too much credit and quite frankly way too much power. I have seen very brilliant, talented leaders go from being excited about their wild and awe-inspiring dreams to letting one single cynic's voice hurl them to the floor, depressed and ready to give up. They can be at 72, down to -20 degrees, back up to 72, and then as high as 100 degrees. This type of fluctuation will not serve them, or you, well if you want to reach your goals.

To succeed you must not base your decisions on how you *feel*. You must move forward in confidence on what you *know*, that deep-down "fire," the *vision* you got from the *beginning* when you decided to stop crawling and committed to *take flight*. Remember, there is no more crawling once you have transformed, so remove the *feelings* and work from *commitment*. We either believe God placed the dreams inside of us and will see us through or we don't. So stay 72.

"Such a person is double minded and unstable in all they do" – (James 1:8).

Those individuals who aim to accomplish the REMARKABLE are the ones who are clear in their mind first and have made a promise to themselves to be ALL IN no matter what the "naysayers" declare.

Do you know that Walt Disney was fired by his editor because "he lacked imagination and had no original ideas?" Disney even went bankrupt one time, but he still moved forward because he had a *fire* inside of him and nobody could put it out because it was *God inspired*. He was turned down hundreds of times by the so-called "financial experts." Can you imagine what the naysayers said about his dream of two mice becoming icons to the world? Today, Walt Disney Company rakes in $50 billion in revenue yearly.

Hmmm, so much for the "experts." Walt Disney was beyond brilliant, had an imagination second to none, and original ideas that were God inspired to bless the world. Be assured that his legacy of *belief* and *dreaming big* will encourage people of all ages for centuries to come.

I think one of the most inspirational stories of a champion is Bethany Hamilton. Bethany started surfing as a very young child and she loved the ocean from the beginning. This young dreamer, at the age of 13, was attacked by a shark and lost her left arm. Bethany could have allowed all the "fearful naysayers" to paralyze her with all the reasons why she should stop following her "passion," but she IGNORED THE NOISE and "followed her fire." This young woman chose to rise up and get back on her surfboard just 2 years after the attack. Hamilton won first place in the Explorer Women's Division of the National Scholastic Surfing Association National Championships. This champion chose to SHINE, and that is exactly what you should do from this moment on.

I believe every, single naysayer we encounter on our journey provides us an opportunity to SHINE. The darkest days in my life have been my greatest moments to SHINE in the face of adversity. We can "rise up" when we have setbacks and disappointments or we can lie down and quit. It's our choice because it's our "fire." I believe when we RISE up and SHINE it unleashes an enthusiasm that is contagious. It instills a hope within those around us to never give up because they realize they can WIN too. *Brave Inspires Brave!*

When we let our light shine it encourages others to see their way out of darkness, and this can inspire even the most "pessimistic" individual to dare to dream again.

The naysayers don't begin with a defeatist mind-set; their doomsday philosophy was formed by the negative words that were spoken to them. If you are swayed by a naysayer, you allow a vicious cycle to be passed on. You must be brave enough to pursue your dreams with a childlike faith and declare war on the "noise."

"First they ignore you. Then they laugh at you.
Then they fight you. Then you WIN." – Gandhi

CHAPTER 5

The Strategic Plan

Bob Williamson

So far we have discussed:

- Developing healthy self-esteem

- Believing that you can succeed

- Having passion for what you choose to undertake

- Overcoming the naysayers and following the vision in your heart

The next logical step is to develop a strategic plan of action. This is very important and, in fact, there is an old saying about it that I really like:

"Failing to plan is planning to fail. If you don't know where you're going, you will never get there."

Having a well-thought-out comprehensive strategic plan is like having a GPS device that will guide you to the precise location that you desire to visit. It shows where you are currently located, the route you need to take to get to your destination, milestones you will encounter along the way, and how long it will take you to get there. All you need to do is add in the cost of the venture and you have the basic elements of a strategic plan.

Defining Success

Before we launch into a discussion of how to design a plan to obtain success, it would be beneficial to define it.

The dictionary states success as: *"The achievement of something planned or attempted, especially an impressive accomplishment such as the attainment of wealth, fame, power, or achieving a major feat."*

Personally I don't believe in that definition, because I know of too many people who are wealthy, powerful, famous, and have achieved all sorts of accomplishments and yet are utterly miserable. Whitney Houston comes to mind. She was beautiful, a gifted singer and performer who sold hundreds of millions of her records, accumulated megamillions of dollars, owned private jets, yachts, grand mansions, and every material thing anyone could want. She had adoring fans on practically every continent, she was nominated for an Academy Award, Grammys, and assorted music awards too numerous to list.

A friend of mine used to live next door to her and husband Bobby Brown in Atlanta, and he told me that the police were at their house often, breaking up fight after fight. Sadly, despite having everything the world could offer, her life ended when she tragically drowned in a bathtub in Hollywood. An autopsy report later revealed that her body was full of many different illegal drugs. By all accounts at the time of her death, she was miserable, divorced, and alone. Heartbreakingly, her daughter, Bobbi Kristina, eerily endured the same fate a couple of years later when she overdosed and drowned in a bathtub in Atlanta. She was on life support for months, but despite the medical profession's best efforts, she died.

Yes, Whitney Houston was one of the "beautiful people," gifted beyond the galaxy, and she attained wealth, power, fame, and great achievements, but no thinking person who considers Whitney and her daughter's deaths could believe that her life was an acceptable definition of success. Despite all the money, power, fame, and accomplishments she garnered, she was miserable. Her brief life and her daughter's both ended in tragic failure. Who would have ever thought she would end up in such a state?

It is impossible to remain happy all the time!

We often hear: *"I just want to be happy. If I could only be happy."* So is being happy a good definition of success?

One moment you can be happy, and then someone close to you will die, or perhaps you will face some terrible financial or medical situation, or a child or grandchild will go astray. Suddenly you experience the opposite of happiness, and you reach for something beyond this world and all that is in it. The old saying that there are no atheists in foxholes suddenly resonates as we look to our Lord for help.

Imagine that you succeed wildly and attain all those things for which you fought so hard and suddenly you realize that it isn't what you thought it might be. Tom Brady, star quarterback for the New England Patriots, referenced this phenomenon right after winning his second Super Bowl ring. Reporters excitedly asked how he felt about winning this tremendous honor, not once but twice. He puzzled most everyone in attendance by dejectedly replying, *"Somehow I thought it would mean more than this."* A handsome, gifted athlete with a supermodel wife, money, fame, millions of admirers and adoring fans, and accomplishments galore, including TWO Super Bowl victories, learned (as so many of us have) that nothing this world has to offer, no material thing, no amount of money, no accomplishment will fill that hole in your heart apart from a close relationship with our Savior.

Abraham Lincoln thought that happiness is a state of mind that can be controlled, declaring: *"Most folks are about as happy as they make up their minds to be."* With all due respect to ol' Honest Abe, that is simply not accurate. *Life consists of happy and sad times.* Both are temporary conditions and, like it or not, we'll taste them equally as we careen through life (regardless of attitude).

- We celebrate new life and we grieve life taken away.

- We are victorious and we go down in defeat.

- We laugh and we cry.

- We smile and we suffer.

- We win and we lose.

- We rise and we fall.

- We are young and we get old.

- We enjoy health and we lose it.

- We start out young, thin, and taut, and end up old, plump, and wrinkled, LOL.

Happiness is actually an emotion that we experience as we go through life and is always temporary. It is directly related to whatever is currently happening to us. When things are good and we get what we want, we feel happy. On the other hand, when things go bad and disappoint, we feel sad.

Some remain perpetually frustrated because they want to remain happy no matter what. Like the restless ocean with its constant movement, we search the world hoping to find something that will fill the void in our lives as we desperately yearn for happiness. We try many different avenues only to discover:

- We won't find it in a bank account, because money can't buy it—just ask anyone who has money.

- We won't find it in a fleeting moment of pleasure in a bedroom, because it's gone before we know it.

- We won't find it by getting smashed in a barroom, because soon we'll be nursing a headache and bad taste in our mouth.

- We won't find it through participation in some thrill-seeking adventure or major accomplishment; when it's over, the thrill will be gone and forgotten, burned away like the early morning fog.

- We won't find it by owning a private jet, boat, limo, diamond ring, grand home, or any material thing; once the novelty wears off, those are just things.

- We won't find it in our family, boss, coach, teacher, pastor, leaders, or best friend; they are frail human beings just like us and will eventually disappoint.

- We won't find it when we take some magic happy pill, do a line of cocaine, suck on a crack pipe, smoke a joint, or stick a needle in our arm; when it wears off we will want more and more and more, and get less and less and less.

- We won't find it in a great career, being famous, or by being a renowned CEO; it is at best a fleeting moment in time and will soon be forgotten.

- We won't find it in physical beauty or buff bodies, because soon enough that will fade and wilt away like a freshly cut flower in a hot desert sun.

These will initially offer some form of limited pleasure and happiness, but none are permanent. Ultimately happiness cannot be defined as success, because when the temporary pleasure is gone and it fades, invariably the question must be asked: *"Is this all there is?"*

If happiness isn't success, then what is?

Thomas Jefferson wrote: *"Success is to be loved by children and respected by intelligent men and women."* A friend of mine recently told me that he felt that I had achieved that worthy distinction in this life.

Some, including me, would say that even if I could achieve such a worthy and noteworthy accomplishment, it is far too shallow a definition and is hardly deserving of a declaration of true "success."

Well what about the wealth, power, fame, and great achievements I've realized? I would simply say that they are without question credible and worthy, and at times have given me a tremendous degree of happiness and satisfaction; however, none of them, in and of themselves or all together, can deliver everything I desire on a permanent basis and therefore cannot demonstrably prove that I'm a "success."

This dilemma reminds me of the lyrics to the Rolling

Stones hit song "Satisfaction." These rock stars had mesmerizing charisma and tremendous talent, and it earned them all that the world has to offer, including, fame, women, material things, adoration, and power, and yet they screamed into the microphone:

I can't get no satisfaction,
I can't get no satisfaction.
'Cause I try and I try and I try and I try.
I can't get no, I can't get no satisfaction
No satisfaction, no satisfaction, no satisfaction.

One thing is certain, success isn't to be defined in the manner that most of us in this world are attempting to define it.

True Definition of Success is Peace, Joy, and Love

My definition of genuine success is the achievement of peace, joy, and love in one's life. The bottom line is that you can know this kind of success living modestly in a mobile home, or in a grand mansion like a king. Material things are not the measure of success. No material thing can fill our souls with what they need. In my experience, true success can only come from God. I've personally observed that the peace, joy, and love of God never fade much less dies, even when faced with horrendous trials and tribulations. It is the best definition that I can come up with for success.

With that said, I was fortunate to learn that it is not an "either/or" choice. Attaining some of the pleasures of this world *plus* having a wonderful relationship with our Creator is readily achievable and I believe within God's plan for us.

If I had to choose just one, however, it would be having that marvelous relationship with my Creator. The Apostle Paul summarized my thoughts on this subject when he said,

"Everyone who competes in the games trains with strict discipline. They do it for a crown that is perishable, but we do it for a crown that is imperishable."

Our Creator wants us to succeed in life and is prepared and willing to help us achieve the things that we want, provided that they are within His will for our lives. He will not bless our becoming the leader of a prostitution ring or drug cartel, but He will bless those wholesome endeavors in life that are within His will for us. I know that God does not desire for anyone to fail, and I think He wants us to abundantly enjoy life and all that He has created for us. As the old adage states, *"We can have our cake and eat it too."* I would simply add, one last time, that our primary focus should be on Him, and not the lusts of the world.

Even when we transition from happiness to sadness and suffering, He will always be there for us. Success does not flee from sad times, rather it *engages* them, just as it does with our happy times. Success must be all-encompassing, because happy and sad times are both parts of our lives.

An excellent illustration of this can be found in the Holy Bible, which states that, *"For the joy set before Him, Jesus endured the cross."* Jesus had just prayed so intensely that he sweated blood as he lay facedown in the Garden of Gethsemane calling upon God to help Him. He was preparing Himself for the painful torture and cruel death that He knew He would soon willingly endure on the cross. His task was to take upon Himself the punishment for the sins of the *entire world* in order that we might be reconciled with our Holy God.

No one in their right mind would think Jesus was *happy* about knowing His incomprehensible agony would begin in just a few short hours; however, Jesus Christ looked out into the future far beyond His personal suffering and agony. He knew that because of His sacrifice, death would be defeated, and those of us who would choose to follow Him would have the opportunity to enjoy everlasting life.

We were on His mind that day as He anticipated the new beginning that He would create. Despite looming disaster, He felt peace, joy, and love because His children would soon be bathed, cleansed, and purified in His loving glory, healed and made perfect by His blood sacrifice and stripes. And He knew that after it was finished, we could be allowed to be with Him, and enter His rest and enjoy His gentle peace in paradise for eternity. And forevermore His loving grace would erase all tears, sadness, sickness, misery, and death, and sin would never again stand between His children and Him. Even in His darkest hour His absolute love provided Him with sheer joy and incomprehensible peace.

His example should fill each of us with hope and serve as a valuable lesson.

Jesus Christ demonstrated the purest definition of success when He accomplished a noble and just purpose despite the worst this world could muster against Him. And He managed all this in a humble and loving spirit of peace, sheer joy, and absolute love, even asking that His Father forgive those who mocked and spat on Him and unjustly took His precious life.

How we can find success in our own lives

We should understand that it is impossible to succeed in life alone. It requires supernatural strength to endure painful trials, and that strength can only be obtained through Christ. This is verified for us in Romans 8:28,

> *"And we know that God causes everything to work together for the good of those who love God and are called according to his purpose for them."*

This plainly states that *God* is the one who makes everything work together for good; not us! Believe this verse! Memorize it.

Are You Willing to Pay the Cost?

Before you launch into what will be a time-consuming endeavor of developing a written plan, you first have a decision to make. Success always comes at a cost and you must decide whether you're willing to pay that cost? Colin Powell said it well when he offered: *"A dream doesn't become reality through magic; it takes sweat, determination, and hard work."* Not surprisingly, the greatest inventor of all time, Thomas Edison, stated, *"Genius is 99 percent perspiration and 1 percent inspiration. I never did anything worth doing by accident, nor did any of my inventions come indirectly through accident, except the phonograph. No, when I have fully decided that a result is worth getting, I go about it, and make trial after trial, until it comes."*

Let's pretend that your noble and worthy purpose in life is to make tons of money so that you can give large amounts away to great causes—as well as enjoy the good life.

In order to fund your ambition in a mighty way, you have

decided that the quickest and perhaps only way to get there aside from hitting the lottery is to found and build your own business. Like all entrepreneurs, you will soon realize:

- You will put in exceedingly long, difficult, and stressful hours.

- You will undoubtedly be stuck at work and slaving away while your buddies party away.

- You will most certainly spend time away from family; something your spouse and kids will be none too happy about.

- You will probably have to work for months and even years with little or no salary, and sacrifice many of the comforts of life that your cohorts enjoy.

- You will be discouraged by many people, including family members who will ridicule your ideas and dreams and share grim statistics like 11 out of 12 businesses fail.

- You will daily incur the risk of your business failing and losing everything you own.

- You will be tempted to quit when the going starts getting tough (and it will).

So why would anyone in his right mind want to embark on a course such as this? Because we want to change the world, reach for the pot of gold at the end of the rainbow, do something significant, and make our indelible mark on this life.

The wonderful thing about America is that that we don't have to be geniuses to succeed, and regardless of gender, ethnicity, age, religious preference, or social standing we can make our dreams a reality—including *changing the world*—provided we are willing to pay the price.

Are you willing to pay that price for success in your life?

So about now you are probably thinking that I should tone down the hyperbole and not exaggerate. *Change the world?* Yeah, right!

Not convinced? Let's look at changing the world in real numbers. Did you know that if you were to change just 10 people, and subsequently they were to change 10, and then those people would change 10, and so on, in just five generations 800 million people (twice the U.S. population) would be changed? Add another generation and 8 billion would be changed, which exceeds the current population of the world.

Hmmm, doesn't seem too difficult now, eh?

But what if changing the world is not your thing, and instead you merely desire to accomplish something meaningful in your lifetime? Well meaningful accomplishments come at a price too. Consider the dreams of an athlete who wants to become an Olympian and what the training regime looks like. To achieve this level, athletes train for hours each day; they work out whether they are tired, sore, sick, it is their birthday, all their friends are off having fun, good mood, bad mood, whatever. The cost to them is worth it; they dream of one day standing on that podium with the entire world watching as they receive their gold medal. The pain is worth the gain.

Is it to you?

Impossible to Fail

Maybe before you answer this question you are thinking, "What if I expend all that energy working long, hard hours and I sacrifice my free time and money, and still fail? What if I don't make it?

Don't make it?

Don't make it?

Are you kidding me?

Sometimes no matter how hard you try, you cannot succeed at an endeavor; however, by the mere act of *trying*, you do not fail. Most people won't even dare to try. Listen to what Theodore Roosevelt wrote:

> *"It is not the critic who counts; not the man who points out how the strong man stumbles, or where the doer of deeds could have done them better. The credit belongs to the man who is actually in the arena, whose face is marred by dust and sweat and blood; who strives valiantly; who errs, who comes short again and again, because there is no effort without error and shortcoming; but who does actually strive to do the deeds; who knows great enthusiasms, the great devotions; who spends himself in a worthy cause; who at the best knows in the end the triumph of high achievement, and who at the worst, if he fails, at least fails while daring greatly, so that his place shall never be with those cold and timid souls who neither know victory nor defeat."*

So what is the measure of your heart? Do you have the will to succeed? Can you summon up the necessary courage to be your very best in those dark moments that are discouraging and painful? Can you envision yourself standing in the winner's circle?

You should consider the cost prior to entering the arena. *But don't begin until you count the cost* Luke 4:28, and keep in mind that you need not enter the battle alone. The power of hope that is found in Philippians 4:13, *"I can do all things through Jesus Christ who strengthens me,"* should remain foremost in our minds. Understand that the Lord loves us and wants us to succeed and doesn't desire for anyone to fail. When we combine His love and strength to our personal attributes, character, and self-discipline and link it with our network of loyal friends and the team of supporters we have systematically built, then we realize we are not alone in our struggle, and it becomes more achievable.

Those who make it to the winner's circle will be individuals who tenaciously maintain their faith as they persevere through the dark trials and look beyond the pain, discomfort, discouragement, and frustrations to that glorious day when they are standing in the winner's circle reaping their just reward. They will believe in themselves, their ideas, and their God, and will work through any pain using the example of Jesus Christ as their model.

So finally you must consider the cost versus the gain, and if you deem it to be worth the effort, then go for the prize with all you've got! Take it from me, it will be well worth the effort.

Begin with the End

I learned early in my business career to never begin a new venture without first considering the end, (or to use a more common term, develop an "exit strategy"). By seeing where I wanted to end up, I could plan accordingly to find a way to meet my objective of getting there. When you begin to formulate a vision of what success looks like, it will be worth the effort to spend time planning for how you can finish well.

So I unabashedly say that outlining your vision "beginning with the end" is of paramount importance. Whatever it is that you choose to do, spend the necessary time to find a way to finish well. Be a long-term thinker; I have been called an "eternity thinker" by more than one: This means keeping the things of the world in context and realizing that actuarially the average life span of a human being is currently 79.9 years old. But eternity is forever. Obviously, we should be thinking more about how eternity will be spent than this relatively short period on earth.

Be willing to fight the good fight and focus on finishing well.

For the purposes of this overview I would be remiss in not giving you some pointers in preparing a brilliant plan that will beat the odds and enable you to live your dream.

Market research

I've never started a business for which I didn't conduct market research. You will need to do this, and should plan on it. Before launching any idea, I recommend that you first find out for sure whether there are enough potential customers out there to make your venture viable.

If indeed there is a tremendous need for your product or service, determine if anyone else is already providing it. You might have thought that "you invented the wheel," but others came up with the same idea long ago.

If there's a business already in that arena, how well is it doing? Find out its strengths and weaknesses by conducting a competitive analysis, and do it on all competitors in that space. Personally, I would never begin a company unless I felt I could (in time) become number one in the industry or number two at the very least.

What you will likely find is that, yes, someone else is already doing something like what you envision. It is extremely difficult to come up with an idea that has not already been explored, but in many cases it is not that difficult to compete and, in fact, "blow the competition out of the water" by excelling in all that you do.

Every company has strengths and weaknesses. Learn from them. Do all that your competitors are doing well and improve upon those areas where they falter. If they have a great idea, then adopt it as your own and look for ways to improve upon it. I've learned from my competitive analysis that "*imitation is much less expensive than innovation,*" and there is no need to reinvent something that works extremely well. Use that as your starting point, and then work earnestly to improve in all areas, particularly customer service.

Money and budget

Understand the cost-price equation. You cannot spend more than you take in and survive for long. Is there ample demand for the product or service at a price that will produce a profit for the company? Either the math works or it doesn't. Better to do this on paper than by experimentation using your hard-earned money.

Poor accounting can ruin a business quicker than anything. You cannot control a business if you don't know what is going on financially. Do not believe that an accounting firm hired primarily to do the taxes will keep watch over the business. If you think yes, then you are mistaken. Accountants are rarely entrepreneurs themselves, and while they are adept at doing taxes, few are qualified to give solid advice on running your business. In reality, it is the job of the chief financial officer to provide meaningful numbers to the business owner. Many start-up entrepreneurs will have to perform this task themselves until it becomes affordable to hire a CFO. If you do not possess accounting skills, then plan for that when determining your capital contribution needs. *You cannot ignore it; this is an axiom, (law).*

No business can function without funding. Think of it as the oxygen that fuels an organism. Remove the oxygen and the organism dies. You will need to build some cash reserves. Business is cyclical, and bad things can and will happen. Cash cures many ills: the loss of an important customer, a lawsuit in this sue-happy nation, the loss of a "dream maker" employee, or a campaign against a competitor who might be coming on strong. These things can throw a well-conceived budget into a tailspin, especially if you've reached your borrowing limit.

Once when bringing my big boat into a marina, an old

"salty-dog" boat captain advised me: *"Go slow so you look like you know!"* He warned me to idle into the marina and alternate between putting the engine into gear and taking it out in order to dock with ease. There have many foolish captains who have come roaring into a marina in true "hot dog" fashion, expecting to throw the boat into reverse at the last moment, only to have something go awry and instead plow into a dock.

This phrase applies to business as well. *Go slow so you look like you know.* Some sage advice for you is that *bigger is sometimes better, but profitable is always good,* especially cash profits as opposed to "book" profits. Growing too fast increases the need for more and more cash, and if your neck is stretched way out there and catastrophe hits, you just might lose your head. Out-of-control growth and overexpansion have ruined more than one successful business. Sometimes less is really more. *Go slow so you look like you know.* Patiently build a sound profitable company using a comprehensive budget.

Team and leadership

Someone wisely said great companies consist of great people. I would add that great companies and great people are led by *great leaders*. Dysfunctional leaders cannot focus on the vision or the mission. They flit around like darting hummingbirds going from flower to flower, changing the plan from day to day. Most employees dislike instability and insecurity, and constantly changing directions can devastate morale. And while small companies have the advantage over large ones to change direction in rapid fashion, it should be the exception rather then the rule. If you change the plan daily, it cannot be a very well-thought-out plan.

Sometimes the owners or the executive team are the problem and not the solution. Big egos can stifle creativity in employees. Some are so risk-averse that they stop great ideas like they've hit a concrete barrier. Owners are just people, and sometimes people are greedy, insecure, nonconfrontational (as in needing to be liked by everyone, including those who take advantage at every opportunity). Some are sloppy; others are perfectionists to a fault.

No one is a master of all things. We need to perform where we excel and hire others to take over tasks where we lack proficiency. And we need to ALLOW THEM TO DO THEIR JOBS!

When developing a written plan, take all of this into consideration. Put it down on paper and follow it using daily, weekly, monthly, quarterly goals and milestones. Your plan should be used every day. I would not think of beginning my day without referring to a written schedule.

Remember, no successful business owner would consider running a business without a strategic plan. It would be like a builder trying to construct a building without a blueprint. If you don't know where or how to start, Google is a friend when it comes to learning to develop a business plan.

Get started on yours today!

BOB WILLIAMSON AND JAMIE VRINIOS

CHAPTER 5

The Strategic Plan

Jamie Vrinios

A dreamer with no vision is fantasizing; however, a dreamer who has a VISION understands that vision demands a plan to succeed. Those who fail to plan are planning to fail, so developing a strategy to WIN is without question imperative to your success. A vision is your destination, and you must be intentional in your daily activity if you plan to arrive.

Let me ask you, "Where are you going and what is your estimated arrival time?"

You will want to write down your vision and make your plan clear, and if the wind doesn't blow in the direction you were expecting you must be adaptable. The likelihood of unforeseen obstacles thrown into your well-thought-out plan is just an opportunity to adjust your sails and adapt along the way. Keep in mind, trial and error is part of the learning curve to success, so suspend rigid thinking, because it will choke off any creativity necessary to achieve your goals.

Marilyn, my mentor, always reminded me that "too much thinking can make you stinking," so keep that in mind as you develop your plan. A vision with a plan is intentional and rooted in daily disciplined activity, not wishful thinking. If you have made the decision to be ALL IN, then you will see your dreams manifest into reality, provided you are willing to follow principles that are proven to help you succeed.

Are you directionally challenged concerning your goals, or do you KNOW where you are going? Personally, I am directionally challenged when it comes to driving, LOL. I can get lost if I don't have great directions (or better yet, OnStar), but regarding my goals I am CLEAR and always have a PLAN in place. When it comes to driving, I am very THANKFUL for modern GPS-driven technology—it has saved me from a lot of frustration in finding my destination. A plan is no different regarding your vision. Individuals who know where they are going are CONFIDENT, and it is evident in their demeanor and the action they take.

I love this story about Billy Graham:

Billy Graham once told about the time he was visiting a small town when he stopped to ask a little boy directions to the post office. After receiving them, Mr. Graham invited the boy to come to his Crusade that evening. "You can hear me telling everyone how to get to heaven," he told the boy. The little boy's response, "I don't think I'll be there mister, because you don't even know your way to the post office."

This is a funny story but truth lies within it—you must know where you are going if you want to succeed in life.

Imagine for a moment that you would love to take a trip to Hawaii. Will you just dream about this trip of a lifetime, or will you actually make a plan and immerse yourself completely in the nonnegotiable goal of vacationing in this beautiful paradise? You would first make the decision to go, right? Your enthusiasm about the trip should inspire you to find a way or make a way, even if the finances, busy schedule, or other factors may not be there. Correct? If you really want to go, you should just figure it out. To take this adventure, everything must be thought out: dates, finances, location, airline, sightseeing, and, of course, your travel companions.

I think one of my most difficult decisions regarding travel is what to pack, LOL. The same principle applies to our vision. There are those things we must take with us on our journey but many things we should leave behind. Determining necessities from the beginning and not loading up on superfluous items makes for a more pleasant journey. When we apply this mind-set to our goals, it becomes much easier to reach them.

A vision inspires us to develop a plan, and it also dictates the environment we choose, the schedule we create, the books we read, the choices we make financially, and the multitude of sacrifices we are willing to make to get there. I believe it starts as a picture in our mind FIRST. If we BELIEVE IT and SEE IT in our MIND first, we fully commit to do whatever it takes to make it happen.

> *Your beliefs become your thoughts,*
> *Your thoughts become your words,*
> *Your words become your actions,*
> *Your actions become your habits,*
> *Your habits become your values,*
> *Your values become your destiny.*
> *– Gandhi*

I remember when the struggles in my life were so severe it became imperative for me to focus on the vision in my mind of a brighter future in order to summon the courage to continue. I recall the nights it was 10 degrees outside and our home was freezing because I couldn't afford to get the power back on in time for bed. My two children would be cuddled up with me in the bed and I would tell them stories of greater things to come. They had no idea we were broke or of the concerns that were rushing through my mind of how I would pay the bills.

The tears that I cried and prayers that were said while they peacefully slept were continuous. The nights the house had no heat, I would hang a blanket in between two rooms, light a kerosene lamp, and "pretend" we were camping. I wasn't willing to give in to what was going on right in front of me, because the VISION I had imprinted in my mind was much STRONGER than my circumstances.

In my mind my circumstances were temporary and subject to change at any moment, which gave me the COURAGE to NEVER cave in. I was going someplace better in my mind and I just wasn't willing to entertain the second thought. If you have a vision with a plan, it removes all the exit signs and leaves you no room to consider the second thought. If you start to doubt, you should return to what you wrote down and remind yourself of the VISION.

This is why the very first step in planning must be to paint a SOLID PICTURE in your mind, and then you need to write it down in detail. The years when my children were small and I was building my business we would create goal posters at the beginning of every month. They would put swing sets, bikes, dollhouses, drum sets, and even Disney World on their posters as their goals. Whatever dreams our little family had were eventually pasted on our goal posters. I would paste the home I wanted to build for them and the life I wanted to give to them. Every day when I walked into my office or looked at the refrigerator and bathroom mirror, my dreams and my children's were right in front of my face.

How can we formulate and accomplish goals if we omit writing down the very things we desire for our children and ourselves? TRUTH IS, WE CAN'T!

This is why affirmations are so powerful and vital to your strategy. Do you know that everything I ever wrote down and committed to I have achieved, and today there are things on my dream board that will manifest in due time?

"And the Lord answered me: "Write the vision; make it plain on tablets, so he may run who reads it" – (Habakkuk 2:2).

When you begin with the end in mind and set an action plan, you can work backward and set smaller goals that propel you toward your vision. We want to create daily wins. They will, without question, help build the momentum that is necessary to WIN.

A plan should be broken down into yearly, quarterly, monthly, weekly, and then daily goals. It is the daily effort and series of smaller wins that create catalytic movement and lend great power toward achieving the greater goal. I have worked with leaders who set audacious goals, but when it came to developing a plan they put down on paper, they realized for the first time that it may take more time than they'd thought. Writing it down is crucial for someone to understand so they don't set unrealistic expectations.

I am a BIG THINKER, but I have learned that my goals are something I must be willing to work hard for. And you must adopt a similar mind-set from the start. I have always measured the cost of every goal I set, and I encourage you to do the same as you develop your plan.

"But don't begin until you count the cost. For who would begin construction of a building without first calculating the cost to see if there is enough money to finish it?" – (Luke 14:28).

I don't think this verse refers only to money, and when you set the goal it should stretch you, and I mean really stretch you, to attain it with consistent effort.

A goal that is unrealistic will only discourage you, so from the beginning you will want to weigh the cost. Are you willing to put the time and effort in that is required to reach your goals? "Success doesn't come at bargain prices" so be willing to pay the price of success. When you break your goals down into WEEKLY MARKERS and then DAILY WINS, it is easy to create your schedule around your nonnegotiable daily activity.

A leader with a passionate vision is willing to clear the calendar for their goals and dreams because it is a main priority in their life. Keep a list of the six most important things you need to accomplish the next day on your nightstand and adjust it daily. When we are in pursuit of our goals, keeping that list in front of us is crucial because unforeseen things just happen along the way and if we don't focus we could easily be distracted.

A list of priorities keeps us focused when distractions come. This list will help you stay on track as you navigate through daily obstacles. Remember, when the mind is made up and you are committed, the evidence will be found in your calendar. If I could see your phone and calendar I would be able to tell very quickly what your priorities are— we invest our time in what we value. Make sure your time is invested wisely toward the top priorities that will lead you to your goals, because we will never get more than 24 hours in a day.

Procrastination is a cancer to any dream, so as you are prioritizing your time, keep in mind that there are good choices for investing your time and then there are the BEST choices. The BEST decisions lead us to our destination, and though the good may be enjoyable in the present, know that they will delay what we desire for the future.

"Procrastination is the bad habit of putting off until the day after tomorrow what should have been done the day before yesterday." – Napoleon Hill

In the beginning, when I was building my business I had to give up weekends with my children short-term so I could have more time with them in the future. I remember sitting them down and explaining to them that I couldn't be at everything for a little while, but soon I would be. We would go back to our goal posters and I would remind them of our dreams. I would reward my children every single time I hit a new goal and we would celebrate, which only inspired me to keep going.

John Maxwell has said that *"We can pay the price now to play later or play now and pay later."* So which will it be? Are you willing to do whatever it takes to see your dreams manifest? Have you set a date on your goals, and if you have, does it stir up a sense of urgency? All of these questions are crucial in designing your strategy, and if you don't ask them, a blueprint to your dreams is useless.

When you set the plan in place you will want to evaluate what you expect from yourself and anyone involved in your vision. I have always looked at my progress at the beginning of the week and the end of the week so I can make any necessary adjustments along the way. If you want to succeed, you must be adaptable and willing to pivot when necessary. Without evaluation, you have no way of gauging your progress. Anything worth building in life will take time, and you must take ownership from the start. And that means, *no matter what*, YOU ARE IN IT TO WIN IT.

We build our future from the bottom up, never the top down, so our plan will always be one step at a time. I would rather see something take a little more time to achieve excellence than to build it frenetically and pray that it holds up when it is finished. Can you imagine planting those wildflower seeds in the ground and telling them to hurry up because you need them to grow?

In today's world people are so impatient with the transformational process that they often give up quickly, and it's such a shame because the pattern they have developed will follow them in every area of their lives. It's easy to look at the highlights of someone's life and say,

"WOW, I would love to achieve that in my life"; however, there was a price that they paid along the way.

Champions are not developed on the day they compete to win. They are conditioned and transformed into champions by showing up every day to practice and by getting knocked down but getting right back up over and over and over again until they succeed.

When you are pregnant with a dream, it will be evident to the world, but the delivery date will vary for each of us. You always know the birth of a dream is about to crown, because you will meet the most resistance in that season and that is your signal to PUSH toward the finish. You can always tell what is inside of a person when pressure is applied. So when it comes, don't give up!

It's your BRAVER-THAN-EVER moment to BREAK THROUGH AND TAKE FLIGHT.

Never compare yourself to others along the way. We tend to compare our weakness to their strengths and become discouraged. In truth, we all have strengths and weaknesses, and human beings tend to observe just the strengths in the superstars. It is imperative that you run your own race and operate from your strengths, where the fire burns the brightest. The plan will keep you on track, but be patient with the process. Any vision worth pursuing transforms us from the inside out.

I came across this story recently and I hope it encourages you as much as it did me:

An elephant and a dog became pregnant at the same time. Three months later the dog gave birth to six puppies. Six months later the dog was pregnant again, and in nine months gave birth to a half dozen puppies. The pattern continued.

On the 18th month, the dog approached the elephant, questioning, "Are you sure that you are pregnant? We became pregnant on the same date. I have given birth three times to eighteen puppies, and they are now grown and have become big dogs, yet you are still pregnant. What's going on?" The elephant replied, "There is something I want you to understand. What I am carrying is not a puppy but an elephant. I only give birth to one baby in two years. When my baby hits the ground, the earth feels it. When my baby crosses the road, human beings stop and watch in admiration. What I carry draws attention. What I'm carrying is mighty and great."

You be like that elephant! Never lose Faith and Never Give Up. What you have inside of you is MIGHTY and GREAT!!

CHAPTER 6

Action

Bob Williamson

You have reached a very important milestone by now:

- You should possess healthy self-esteem.
- You should have a vision and solidly believe that it will succeed.
- You have determined that you will laugh off all the naysayers and follow the vision in your heart.
- You contain unbridled passion for what you have chosen to undertake.
- You have counted the costs, risks, and sacrifices that will be required to achieve excellence and determined that they are well worth it and have developed a strategic plan of action.

Now what?

Now it's time for ACTION!

Well I for one feel like an idiot for writing an entire chapter on how to take action. It seems so unnecessary, but after deep reflection on a lifetime of observing friends and acquaintances who never succeed in attaining their dreams, I am convinced that most never get there because they never go beyond the dreaming stage.

Spending too much time overthinking and doubting yourself and your ideas leads nowhere. Consider this quote by one of the best business leaders of all time.

"You don't have to be great to start, but you have to start to be great." – Zig Ziglar

The inescapable conclusion is not to let fear incapacitate your greatness. Success is just like baking a cake. You can have all the ingredients assembled and ready to go, but unless you start following the recipe and get to cooking, you aren't going to bake anything. It seems like a simple point, but you would be amazed at how many people end up talk, talk, talking, but never get go, go, going!

Have you ever seen a dog chase its tail around and around? They just can't ever succeed at catching it. It reminds me of some of the indecisive people I've met. They just keep circling and circling in frustration.

The same is true in football. A running back who crosses the field from sideline to sideline but doesn't put his head down and drive forward will never carry the ball across the goal line for a touchdown. You don't win games by running in circles or back and forth. You push down the field and force yourself into the end zone. Reading 10 books and Googling for 10 hours about a subject isn't as useful as 10 minutes spent doing it. You simply must take action!

Ask yourself what you are waiting for. Are you waiting for a sure thing? A guarantee that there is zero possibility that you might make a mistake and or fail? If so, you will never begin, because there are no guarantees in life. You just need to grow some courage and get moving.

Taking action is crucial. Many people waffle on a decision, weighing every factor, and seem deathly afraid they will make a mistake. First, that is the mistake, because it accomplishes nothing.

When I come to a fork in the road and simply cannot determine which way to go, I just make my decision and, right or wrong, plunge forward. Numerous times I've reached a point after analyzing a situation from every angle and finding no perfect choice that I, believe it or not, flipped a coin and went for it. Risk is an integral part of life, and one cannot achieve greatness without assuming some risk.

Action forces us to risk being wrong. Okay, so you're wrong about something. That doesn't mean it's the end of the world. I make more mistakes than anyone in my organizations, because I do more than anyone. Mine are generally very expensive mistakes too. But I do more things right than wrong and succeed despite them. I also learn from every mistake and try not to repeat it.

Did you know that millionaires go bankrupt an average of 3.5 times? This tells me that most serious people make serious mistakes along their journey, but they don't give up and learn from them and keep trying again and again until they achieve their goal. Making mistakes just verifies that you are a human being. No one, aside from Jesus Christ, is perfect. We all make them. It is an honest mistake the first time; however, it is a dumb mistake if it's made over and over. The lesson to be learned is that we learn from our mistakes and can use those hard lessons to avoid making them the next time around. Don't be a victim of the worst mistake *fear* which causes you to fail to take action.

Another reason for failing to act is indecisiveness due to a fear of failure. As Zig Ziglar would say, "Get that *stinking thinking* out of your head." In the first place, you need to understand that because you are attempting to accomplish your project, you cannot fail. The mere act of tackling something grand is success. Most folks are too timid and lack the moxie to so much as *try* something bold that might smell like risk. What they don't realize is that all of life is risk. There are no guarantees.

I once owned a huge mail-order business and consequently spent millions of dollars on printing. I met a man who was a part-time printing broker, and he would arrange all my printing needs for a small percentage. He worked full-time at the post office and on the side opened a small print shop in a shopping center as a second job. He would print what he could at his little shop and broker out the bigger jobs.

This guy was phenomenal. I counseled him one day and told him he should just quit his postal job and go into the printing business full-time. My work alone would provide a large foundation to get him going, and with customer service like he provided I could not see a problem in him garnering other clients and wildly succeeding.

He had a look of terror in his eyes and told me of the many benefits from his post office job and its stability, and his wife's concerns, yada, yada, yada. It took almost a year to finally convince him, but finally he took my advice. The last time I visited him he had a 100,000-foot printing plant loaded with numerous million-dollar printing presses, and he was thanking me from the bottom of his heart for continuing to encourage (and cajole him) into making the leap that led to his becoming a multimillionaire.

Remember, vacillating will only disappoint. Go for it!

CHAPTER 6

Action

Jamie Vrinios

*"It is not the dreamers that are remembered,
it's the doers."* – Tim Tebow

Do you really WANT success? I've asked countless numbers of people if they WANT success and they reply with a resounding YES! However, when it actually comes down to the sacrifices required to attain success there is only a small percentage who choose to break out of their oh-so-cozy cage. If you WANT to succeed it will be evident in your ACTION. Action is what separates a dreamer from the doer.

This story gives such a vivid illustration of what it means to WANT success. So my question to you is, do you really WANT it?

There was a man who wanted to know the secret of success, and sought the answer from a guru. Now this was a wise, old sage who knew every secret of life. He lived in isolation on a mountaintop. The man set out on a long and difficult journey to meet this wise man. He was determined to reach the top and had to overcome many obstacles along the way. He fought through thick forests, scaled huge boulders, escaped wild beasts, and at last he clambered to the peak of the mountain and laid on the ground, gasping for breath. A few minutes later, he sat up and beheld the guru seated beside him in deep meditation.

Silently, he waited. Almost an hour later, the guru opened his eyes and glanced at the man. He raised an inquiring eyebrow.

The man stammered, "Oh wise and all-knowing seer, I come to you in search of the secret of success." The guru didn't reply. He simply stood up and started walking down the hill. The man followed. He found it difficult to keep pace with the old man, who seemed to skip from one rock to the other like a mountain goat. They walked steadily for another hour and he wondered if they were going back to the foothills.

Suddenly, they came upon a clearing. In the middle was a clear lake. The rays from the setting sun glinted softly on the still water. The guru walked up to the edge of the lake and beckoned the man to come closer. With a gesture, he asked him to kneel. Unquestioningly, the man did as the guru ordered. Suddenly, he felt himself being seized by a strong hand at the back of his neck. His head was forced down under the water and held there firmly. "This is some kind of test," said the man to himself as he sat still. A minute passed and he was growing breathless. The grip on his neck hadn't weakened. Another minute crawled by and now he was getting anxious. His heart beat heavily in his chest, his throat tightened, and his lungs screamed for air. He struggled to arise and the old man's grip became even stronger, pressing him further down into the water.

Now, the man was in a panic. He thrashed around wildly, trying with all his energy to loosen the vise around his neck. Precious seconds passed and he felt his strength slowly ebbing away. He thought he was going to die! Just as he was about to give up hope, and rueful of his folly in ever coming here, the hand on his collar let go. Violently leaping onto the shore, the man drew in his breath in heaving gasps. Delicious oxygen flooded his lungs. His vision grew clearer. The hammering in his throat slowed down and his hands stopped trembling.

He felt a deep anger welling up from within him. Standing up, he faced the guru and screamed, "Are you CRAZY? You could have killed me!" The guru simply stared at him for a long moment. Then he spoke for the first time. "You wanted to know the secret of success. Here it is. Do you remember, just a few minutes ago, how badly you wanted to take that next breath of air? When you want success that badly, you will have it. That's the secret of success." Without saying another word, the guru turned around and walked back to the hilltop.

When I first read this story a few years ago, it resonated with my spirit, because I GET IT!!! Anyone who has ever achieved something great even when the herd is shouting IMPOSSIBLE knows EXACTLY what it feels like to be OBSESSED with a DREAM, and not just any dream, THEIR DREAM. I know what it feels like to want something so badly that I was WILLING to do whatever it took to shift my life in the direction of my dreams. I wasn't willing to accept status quo, and neither should you if you want to succeed. Whatever the majority is doing, I would highly encourage you to go the opposite way. You have no chance of seeing your dream manifest if daily ACTION doesn't become an OBSESSION.

It doesn't matter what you have going on. Make a commitment from the beginning that, no matter what, you will take action toward making your dreams become reality every single day. Someone who truly believes in a vision doesn't need to be convinced to take action.

A vision is something that wakes you up and keeps you up because it is your *why*, the *fire in your belly*, your *calling*. It is an OBSESSION. Even if you want to put it down, you can't because it is a permanent fixture in your mind, heart, soul, and spirit. It is what you were created for. Those around you may never get it but that's irrelevant to your success because it's your dream not theirs, and you must take ownership and declare war on any excuse that could prevent you from action.

I wasn't feeling too "great' about my chances of success when I was living as a broke, single mom because I had not taken enough action in my life to move to the level I desired for myself and my children.

My passion and obsession to change my circumstances

far outweighed my insecurity and fear of the unknown, but action was necessary to change my situation.

If you want to succeed, you must activate your faith by executing your plans into action. Your faith will increase the more you exercise it with daily activity. Many may "talk" about goals, dreams, and making a difference in this world, but if there is no action to back it up, their words are useless.

"In the same way, faith by itself, if it is not accompanied by action, is dead" (James 2:17).

When I made the decision to walk away from respiratory therapy and go into medical sales I knew daily disciplined action would be required if I were to succeed in sales. Likewise, when I walked away from my corporate cage to live the life of an "entrepreneur" I knew it demanded MASSIVE ACTION or I would absolutely fail and have to return to the "golden handcuffs" that had restrained me.

I'd invested countless hours into someone else's dream, and it was time for me to BUILD my OWN.

Was I afraid?

Uh, YES, but that is how I became BRAVE—by pushing through the fear and taking ACTION. You must IGNORE THE NOISE if you want to the live the LIFE of your DREAMS. Fear will paralyze you if you allow it into your mind, so don't even give it access.

Beware of the "second thought" that comes into your mind after you make a firm commitment to your crazy dream. The second thought is DOUBT, and it leads to procrastination. The individual who procrastinates is literally allowing fear to overrule faith, and it puts action at a standstill, which delays anything great from manifesting in life. FAITH works in the opposite way, because it will INSPIRE you to keep going even when you don't see it in the natural. Faith and fear will manifest two different outcomes in your life, so you must face your fears and overcome them if you want to WIN.

In the beginning of my career in direct sales I knew if I was going to succeed I had to confront my greatest fear and take action in spite of it. At first, I was allowing other people's opinions to affect me, and by doing that I was giving fear a foothold to deprive me of reaching my goals. The second thought, the DOUBT that was starting to play in my mind, began to paralyze me from wanting to take a chance on myself. I had zero time to waste, so FEAR HAD TO GO! I wanted success so bad that I was willing to lay it ALL down on the line to WIN. I desired transformation in my life so much I was willing to take the RISK. Do you know what my greatest fear was? It was the thought, "What if I fall flat on my face? How will I provide for my children?" The irony was how I could doubt myself, considering everything I had already overcome in my life.

I had overcome poverty as a single mom, so it was ridiculous that I still allowed doubt in my mind. The difference between someone who keeps going and the one who gives up is how long they choose to entertain the doubt and fear. Do you know what I did to confront my fear? I called a friend and said, "I know you think I am crazy for doing this and that's okay, but I really need to know that, if I fail, I can live in your basement with my children for a month while I figure it out."

I was not concerned about losing anything—I was starting from nothing. I just wanted to make sure we would have somewhere to go if I fell flat on my face. I was more afraid of giving up on the fire that was burning bright inside of me than I was of failing. Many people are more afraid of running out than they are of running over when it comes to achieving greatness in their life. I had nowhere to go but up, so that was an advantage in all actuality. Keep in mind I was $100,000 in debt and owned absolutely NOTHING.

The first question I will ask any leader on goal setting is, "If you knew you couldn't fail how big would you dream?" The second question, "If I handed you $1 million how would that impact your choices in life?" If the person I am coaching tells me that upon receiving $1 million they would stop pursuing their goal, dreams, purpose, their calling, their answer speaks a very loud message. The person who stops taking action because they have enough money in their bank account has no vision past their own needs in life. One of my favorite scriptures is,

> *"You are the salt of the earth, but if the salt loses its saltiness, how can it be made salty again? It is no longer good for anything except to be thrown out and trampled under foot"* – (Matthew 5:13).

If we are called to be the salt of the earth, then our vision must extend past our own life in order to be an encouragement to those around us. Even though I wanted to succeed financially, my passion went way beyond just paying the bills and playing it "safe," which is why I was able to take risks. I wanted to show my children that God has a

DESTINY for their life and He has purposed them for something GREAT.

My vision now extends past my family into countless lives because I kept moving forward no matter what the cost. I had creditors calling me DAILY, asking for money that I did not have. But you know what, I chose to IGNORE THE NOISE and keep moving. You must do the same if you want to finish well. The bills would come and I paid what I could. I knew one thing for sure, those bills would be back next month, so any inaction on my part would only make things more severe. I gave myself no other option but to get SOULED OUT and take ACTION. The more action I took the STRONGER my FAITH grew, and my PURPOSE became my OBSESSION. If you allow negative circumstances to paralyze you, then it makes it impossible for you to take the vital action necessary to transform your life.

When the phone would ring, instead of allowing fear to set in I made the decision to RISE UP. This became my motivation for getting out there and doing what had to be done every single day. The formulas and laws of success that I followed daily were proven, so I was never emotional about my action or results. If I didn't do the numbers and follow the success formula could I expect to succeed? The variables that I could control were the ones that I took massive action toward. If I followed the proven success formula by disciplined daily action, it would yield a harvest because I planted enough seed along the way.

People were unpredictable, but my actions were consistent, diligent, and disciplined toward my goals. I had control over how many calls I made, the number of people

I would speak to daily, and most of all, my ATTITUDE. It is no different with your goals in life, so what do you need to change to create a pattern of action that guarantees the finish you are envisioning for yourself?

If I bake brownies and leave out one ingredient, my brownies are not going to taste very good, so as you move toward your dreams you can't pick and choose the parts you like and leave the rest out. The recipe for success requires every ingredient we have discussed in this book if you want to WIN. You can be the most talented person in the world but if you don't take action you will be surpassed by those who do! If you WANT something you must GO GET IT.

"Things may come to those who wait, but only the things left by those who hustle." – Abraham Lincoln

I was not willing to be a spectator on the sideline of life and watch everyone else play in the game. I wanted to be on the field with the WINNERS. Why not me, I would ask myself daily. And why not YOU? I achieved the first pinnacle of success in my business, which only inspired me to keep moving up until I attained my ultimate goal of national sales director. I could never have been prepared for the level of leadership and commitment that this would demand from me if I had not mastered my "feelings" and moved myself into action every single day.

There were many conversations I held with my mentor, Marilyn, but there were three very pivotal YES-or-NO moments that inspired me into ACTION and led me to where I am today in business.

The first conversation was when she told me, "Jamie, we

are as sick as the secrets we keep." Because of that phone conversation I was able to let go and TAKE FLIGHT for the first time in my life because I knew someone BELIEVED in me.

My second pivotal talk came when I was questioning whether I could really become a top director. I was experiencing some growing pains transforming into a new level of leadership from crawling to flying, and I had been offered another job and was wondering if I should cut and run. I will never forget Marilyn's words, "How much is your soul worth, Jamie? Can anyone buy you? And let me ask you another question. Is your life just about money or is it about the purpose God has for your life?" Marilyn told me if I would focus on my purpose and help others, then God would provide the finances. She told me the more I helped others the happier I would become and that what I sent out into the lives of others would always come back to me. Do you know, from that moment on after our call I NEVER entertained another thought of DOUBT regarding my future. I made a decision to really BLOOM where I was planted, and my massive action was the proof that I believed it!

The third, and most transformational, yes-or-no moment would demand massive action after Marilyn asked me to serve her dream. She wanted me to become a national sales director before she retired, and she was just beyond a year out from that deadline. Marilyn asked me to play FULL OUT because her desire was to leave a legacy and she knew that she could trust me to pass it on. I took the action required to do as she asked.

How will you answer the YES-or-NO moments in your life? Will they inspire you into ACTION or will you join the herd and accept the leftovers in life? How does someone say NO to something that they know deep-down inside they are BORN to LIVE OUT LOUD? The answer to that question? The person who really WANTS to succeed in life and make a contribution to others who live past their lifetime will never decline the invitation to TAKE FLIGHT.

> *Here's to the CRAZY ONES. The misfits. The rebels. The troublemakers. The round pegs in the square holes. The ones who see things differently. They're not fond of rules. And they have no respect for the status quo. You can quote them, disagree with them, glorify or vilify them. About the only thing you can't do is ignore them Because they change things. They push the human race forward. And while some may see them as the CRAZY ONES, we see GENIUS. Because the people who are CRAZY enough to think they can CHANGE THE WORLD, are the ONES WHO DO.*

> – Steve Jobs

Bob Williamson and Jamie Vrinios

CHAPTER 7

Warrior Mentality

Bob Williamson

So far we have discussed:
- You should possess healthy self-esteem.
- You should have a vision and solidly believe that it will succeed.
- You have determined that you will laugh off all the naysayers and follow the vision in your heart.
- You contain unbridled passion for what you have chosen to undertake.
- You have counted the costs, risks, and sacrifices that will be required to achieve excellence and determined that they are well worth it and have developed a strategic plan of action.
- You are taking action daily to attain your goals.

The assumption is that you have proceeded through all the topics and have acted and that your project is well under way. You are rocking along, and suddenly disaster strikes. Every direction you look things appear bleak, and you are filled with despair and downright fear. Could this be the end of your dream?

It is a safe bet that every entrepreneur has experienced this situation many times over. It goes with the territory. This is where the sheep get separated from the goats. You either have a warrior mentality that will kick in and it will be *"game on,"* or you will crawl back to your lair to lick your wounds. It is imperative to maintain a warrior mentality if you are to survive in the rough and tumble business environment where you play for real marbles. Someone once said, *"If it was easy everyone would be doing it."* What will get you through those tough times? My experience tells me that maintaining a positive winner's mind-set despite the difficult situations that you will encounter is the answer.

Business-news site Bloomberg reports that eight out of 10 entrepreneurs who start businesses fail within the first 18 months. A whopping 80 percent crash and burn. I contend most could have succeeded if they would have just hunkered down, gritted their teeth, and kept on fighting "until the last dog dies."

I call it possessing a "warrior mentality," and I liken it to being in combat and receiving orders from my commander that I am to take a mountaintop off in the distance as soon as humanly possible. I envision myself pointing to the peak of that mountain and telling my troops, "Ladies and gentlemen, you see that peak over there? I don't care if we have to hack through the jungle, swim a river, scale a sheer cliff, and fight through the hordes of hell that our enemies will send at us, by this afternoon we're going to be sitting atop that mountain in time to watch the beautiful sunset while sipping iced tea in a comfortable lawn chair, and by the way we won't be taking any prisoners."

In other words, "warriors" accomplish their mission in the face of whatever fiery darts the enemy throws at us. We have the attitude that we *can do* and *will do*!

It is essential to keep a positive mental attitude, albeit it is not always the easiest thing in life to do. We all will face serious trials and tribulations and sometimes the situation will appear to be dreadfully bleak and even hopeless. It is in those dark times that you must reach deep down within your inner being and the warrior mentality must kick in.

A close relationship with the Lord and my unswerving faith in Him is where my positive mind-set and warrior mentality is derived. My life's Bible verse is *"I can do all things through Christ who strengthens me"* (Philippians 4:13). This verse does not say that since we serve a loving God that He will never allow His little darlings to fail at anything. No, it states: ***"I"—can do all things..." I means ME.*** We must do our part using our brains and gifts, and after we have expended all our strength and energy He will use His unlimited strength to ensure that we finish well. And I've found, if necessary, He will even carry us across the finish line.

I might also note that the words "ALL THINGS" do not literally mean ALL THINGS. The Bible is referring to all things *within His will for our lives.* Unwholesome endeavors such as owning a house of prostitution or becoming a drug cartel leader are not within His will for anyone's life and He will never bless them. I always pray and ask God if what I am pursuing is within His will for me. Since the Lord does not communicate verbally with me you might ask how I determine His answer. Easy. I cannot know peace if I'm outside the will of the Lord. When on target, however, I feel completely at ease and can sleep like a baby; when I'm off track, I'm miserable.

Back in my consulting days it seemed that client after

client had been so worn down by the difficulties they faced that they viewed their situations as hopeless. As an outsider I could see that they were on the very brink of achieving wild success. Often minor tweaks and minute changes were all that were necessary, but they were just too battle weary, worn out, and disheartened to see it and exert the effort to change the things they needed to change.

It is when things have greatly deteriorated that quitting invades our minds and begins to take over. When I'm dealing with someone who has reached this point, I sometimes send this poem, which I took the liberty of editing a little:

"Don't Quit"

When things go wrong, as they sometimes will,
When the road you're trudging seems all uphill,
When funds are low and the debts are high,
And you want to smile but you have to sigh,
When care is pressing you down a bit,
Rest if you must, but don't you quit.
When you're worried and full of doubt,
Just remember that success is failure turned inside out,
So stick to the fight when you're hardest hit,
It's when things seem worst that you mustn't quit.

– Unknown

Not long ago I was reviewing some of my memorabilia and I stumbled across this little note I had written to myself on a scrap of paper during the embezzlement crisis detailed in Chapter 4. When I wrote it, I'd just finished walking around my empty WASCO warehouse and shattered business and was feeling very discouraged.

"Ode to the Entrepreneur"
The clatter of the empty warehouse rings a
   doomful, sad sound.
Dark and damp, baleful now with closed doors
   and broken windows.
Everywhere I look I see dreams unfulfilled.
Hard work is over; and so it is.
Where are all the well-wishers, the "friends,"
   the admirers? Where did they all get off too?
Failure, the American dream that will haunt you.
Heartbreaking is the crux of failure's sting.
One must recover from such things and fight back
   to the top.

I wrote this to myself decades ago. I remember writing
it like it was yesterday. I was depressed and sad that day and
saw little hope in recovering from this devastating blow, but
as you can tell from the last line, quitting was not an option.
That, my friends, is *Warrior Mentality*.

I didn't quit and I didn't give up. I just hunkered down
and worked my way onward. I did fully recover from this
dilemma and rebuilt my business beyond its former state
without taking bankruptcy, and I repaid every penny (some
$980,000) to every creditor. I now consider this period of
my life to be one of the toughest, but also the single greatest
learning experience of my career, and although it was a
tough lesson at the time, I know that God allowed my
misfortune to better prepare me for bigger and far better
things on down the road.

As I continued looking through my folder of memorabilia I couldn't help but smile when I saw that the very next piece of paper in this old folder was this little nugget that I had written to myself:

When you just can't take it anymore
Turn it over to the Lord
Work don't worry
Don't shoulder the burden alone
Have faith in God!

This was some good advice I put to writing all those years ago, and it is still valid today. Many of us are facing various trials in our lives, but we must keep in mind that there is a God who loves us and will not give up on us. We shouldn't give up on ourselves or our dreams. Rest if you must but don't you quit! No other personal quality contributes to success more than faith in our God, and after that comes passion, tenacious perseverance, and an attitude of work don't worry.

I know all too well what it feels like to be anxious about ever being able to succeed. Back in the early days of my most successful company, Horizon Software International, I was trying very hard to win our first major multimillion-dollar account. It was nearly impossible to sell one of these jumbo deals unless you already had other megaclients to use as references.

The first question clients would invariably ask was, *"What other district as large as mine is using this technology?"*

I would respond with a sheepish grin on my face, *"Well you'll be the first, but I promise that if you go with us, I'll treat you better than my own mama."*

When that happened, I could rest assured that it was akin to pouring ice water into the client's lap. No bureaucrat ever wanted to assume the risk of being first when it came to spending millions of dollars on a new software system.

Nonetheless I kept at it with bulldog determination and a warrior mentality.

Over a period of months, I'd been trying to impress a potential megamillion-dollar client that our software system was a good fit for his entity. The director was disgusted with his existing system and vendor and seemed impressed with my overall enthusiasm, my straightforward genuine approach, and the quality of our products (that I had shown to him time and again during several visits). My over-riding goal was to project an image of complete professionalism for myself and our new company.

I knew it was an uphill battle and it was going to be a doubly tough sale because of the zero-references-his-size issue, combined with the fact that he already had a very bad taste in his mouth from his current vendor (which translated to software-development companies in general). My experience had been that potential customers have a tendency to throw all vendors into the same pot when in that frame of mind. The bottom line was that it was going to be a very tough sale and, if I was to be successful, I had to make the impression of a lifetime.

I finally got him to agree to a major demonstration of live software, and he'd invited nearly 50 members of his staff to view it. Up to this point the number of folks I'd shown the software to at one time was only six or seven.

Wow!

This was the chance I'd been waiting for and I was determined to make the most of it. I prepared for weeks, and the night before the meeting I was up for hours checking and rechecking every last detail of our presentation. In fact, I'm not sure I ever slept that night.

I was dressed "fit to kill" in a spanking new navy blue Armani suit, double-starched monogramed white shirt, new tie, gleaming shoes. My teeth were scrubbed and every hair on my head was perfectly in place.

I was only two minutes from the meeting place, and I saw no reason to leave too early, so about ten minutes prior to my appointment I whispered a quick prayer and out the door I went. As I briskly walked down the sidewalk enjoying the bright sun, blue sky, and crisp air, I walked under a tree and suddenly a bird pooped on my head and partially on my right shoulder. Apparently it was a very large bird and it had been eating very well—there was no shortage of poop and I was "covered" in it.

It was a direct splattering hit!

Aghast, I ran back to my room but discovered that I'd locked the key inside the room.

"Oh, no!" I screamed at the top of my lungs, as I fruitlessly shook the door handle.

To obtain another key, I had to run down to the lobby with bird poop splattered all over my head and the shoulder of my new Armani suit. The clerk took one look at the menacing expression on my face, and in particular my eyes, and must have known better than to even ask about the bird poop all over me. He nervously and quickly handed me my replacement key, and I ran back to the room.

I did not have time to take a shower or change clothes, and I didn't have another suit with me anyway. I used several damp washcloths to remove the poop from my hair, neck, and suit. By now I was completely flustered. I brushed and brushed with the damp cloth as hard and fast as I could to remove the mess, and when I looked in the mirror for the final time, all the color in my face was gone; I left the room pale and completely frantic. I was going to be late for the meeting of a lifetime.

Minutes later, I arrived at the customer site shaken and nervous. I met my software engineer there and as I looked at him I got even more nervous. My employee was not a very appealing sight; he was grossly overweight (morbidly obese and at least 450 pounds). Unfortunately, he was not much of a conversationalist either, but he was our best programmer. I would never have brought him to meet a customer, unless this client wanted a demonstration of the actual system and live data. I did not feel confident with a deal this big showing live software myself. I wanted him there as added insurance in case something went wrong.

Envision this for a moment. Approximately 50 people crowded into a very small room, standing in a semicircle and focusing on a single computer terminal with a chair in front of it (in those days LCD projectors had not been invented). I was standing there trying to smile, but internally my mind was racing and I was frantically wondering if I'd removed all the bird poop from my hair and clothes, and I began to think that I could smell it. I was rattled.

One never knows what will happen during live software demonstrations, and I was hoping and praying that the software would perform well and not lock up or otherwise malfunction. Just then, my 450-pound-plus technician stepped over to the desk to begin the demonstration, and as he tried to sit down, the chair rolled out from under him and he crashed to the floor with a loud thud. I could literally feel the floor shake. He was rolling back and forth flailing, his arms and legs straight up in the air. He was floundering around struggling to get up, but because of his size he could not seem to rise. It was quite a sight.

So much for projecting an image of professionalism!

The potential buyer, me, and several other people were struggling to help him into an upright position so he could get up. After what seemed like an interminable delay, we were finally successful. Aside from his pride, nothing else was damaged. His face was beet red; so was mine. I could see his face and "feel" mine; it was flushed.

Oddly no one laughed; you could've heard a pin drop in that room. I should have said to myself, "I can do all things through Christ who strengthens me! I can do all things through Christ who strengthens me! I can do all things through Christ who strengthens me!" Unfortunately, what I was saying to myself is not fit to be repeated, much less put in print.

I was humiliated, unnerved, and wishing I was anywhere but in that room. I knew the deal was gone like the wind. I had no sign of warrior mentality left in my being and was defeated in my mind.

And of course, it was all in my head. No one at the

meeting knew about the bird poop incident but me, and everyone felt genuinely sorry for the programmer and knew he was embarrassed to no end. Despite everything, we did get through the demonstration flawlessly, the programmer did an excellent job, and we answered all their questions. Believe it or not, in the end we won this account and many more afterward, largely because of this great reference.

I sincerely believe that God was with me every step of the way through this test, (whether I knew it, or had faith during my test, or not). I no doubt let Him down with some of my thoughts, but I was praying to Him also, and I am delighted that He understands my weaknesses far better than I do and most of all forgives me for my mistakes.

The moral of this story is, when it looks as though all is lost, don't give up! We are always closer to succeeding than we can ever imagine at the time, and God is with us always. Laugh with God when you are besieged with trials; it's far better than getting bent out of shape over it. And most important, don't give up prematurely. Call up your warrior mentality and keep right on working through whatever is thrown at you.

One thing we should all do is learn from our mistakes. This incident taught me a valuable lesson that I've taught to others: Don't give up, and keep fighting through the maze.

This reminds me of the period right after the terrorist attacks on September 11, 2001. The entire country was glued to the television, and no one could think about much of anything except those terrorists who dared attack our country and those murdered by them.

The plane that crashed into the Pentagon hit 100 feet

from the office of the Undersecretary of Defense, who I'd visited when I was working on the Department of Defense project. He was spared because he was at the dentist, but his entire staff did not survive.

It was a scary time and no one was concentrating on business. The tremendous loss of American lives, the audacity of those who dared attack us, and the fear that more was to come were on everyone's minds, including those in our company. And the effect hit our sales, which were nonexistent for three full months. We had ramped up our development project for a total rewrite of our software, Horizon One Source, and we were burning through a million dollars a month just in overhead. Something had to give soon because funds were sinking low and debts were mounting high. I called a meeting with our executive council to discuss the problem.

When I walked into that room those seated around our large conference table all had scared shaken expressions on their faces. As I pondered what to say, I was reminded of a scene in a movie about Gen. George Patton. With mortar shells and bombs bursting everywhere, he walked up and down the trenches of the battlefield occasionally stopping to shake hands and ask the scared soldiers crouching in the trenches where they were from. He seemed oblivious to the danger around him, showing no fear as he solidly clamped down on his cigar as he encouraged soldier after scared soldier. His troops responded and were greatly encouraged by his bravery in the face of tremendous pressure and danger.

Like Patton I wanted to encourage the troops and to be sure I would never allow them to see the slightest hint of fear in my eyes. As I looked around the table at them, my life flashed in front of my eyes. I'd seen death, I'd slept on the side of the road and under bridges, hopped freights, been hungry and penniless, fought through addictions, been inside prison, experienced mega embezzlement, fought vicious fights, faced tragedies enumerable, and yet I had not only survived, but thrived, and God had seen me through it all.

I wasn't scared in the least about 9/11. I was mad! I was mad at those murderous terrorist scums who had attacked our country, and I was mad because they were succeeding in disrupting our way of life.

I contemptuously snorted, *"This is nothing! We'll make it through this crisis and look back one day and smile at how we overcame what we are currently facing."* I lit into that executive council with all the vigor that I had. I told them that we would not be defeated. Yes, cowardly bureaucrats were using the attack as an excuse for not conducting business, and they would continue to use it until we convinced them that the time for mourning was over. I banged my fist on the conference table and shouted,

"WE ARE THE UNITED STATES OF AMERICA! WE DON'T LET TERRORISTS DICTATE OUR WAY OF LIFE!

We need to get out there and call on our customers and, if necessary, *camp out* in their offices until they give us a yes followed by a purchase order. We need to renew our sales effort and I'm personally going to lead the charge."

Immediately every expression at the table changed. They no longer had defeated looks on their faces, and all appeared ready for battle, convinced that we were going to win. In order to cope with the money crunch, I instructed each department to reduce their workforce by 15 percent across the board. No department would be immune. It was the first layoff Horizon ever had to initiate. I told them to eliminate all waste. I borrowed lessons learned from my WASCO days and educated them on the rule to either *get by or justify*, because we weren't spending any money on anything unless they could justify it to my personal satisfaction.

I told them I'd worked out a deal to obtain some capital through an equity investor, and it would help bridge us through the crunch and ease our burden somewhat, but we needed tremendous sales. Finally, I told them: *Work—Don't worry*, and soon we'll see our problems disappear.

In a matter of days, it was as though I'd opened a spigot and the orders began flowing again. In a month we were well on our way to recovery and the crisis was behind us. Within a couple of months, we were positioned to rehire those employees who'd been laid off (at least those we wanted to rehire). Eventually I bought out the equity investor and we were completely back to normal. The best thing about this terrible experience was that our leaders were now seasoned by fire and better off for it because now they understood the *warrior mentality*.

Can Warrior Mentality be learned?

Some believe that you are either born with warrior mentality or you are not. Once, I had an employee whose job in part was to arrange software-presentation visits for me. I was going to Kansas City for a large presentation that could result in several million dollars in business, but I wanted a couple of other appointments with smaller potential clients since I had to travel all the way to the Kansas/Missouri area anyway.

Not more than five to 10 minutes after giving the instructions to my employee to call around for additional appointments, he came back and said he couldn't find any takers. Now I was not in a good mood already, so when he delivered this news I gave him my fiercest look and hissed between clenched teeth with my voice rising with every word I choked out, "Okay, well how about this.

*You go back to your office and try again, and this time try as though **your very job depends upon securing some appointments for me, because it does!**"*

His eyes were as big as tangerines as he scurried back to his office. Within minutes he returned and miraculously had found three potential clients for me to visit, two of whom subsequently placed nice orders. I found that I never had to revisit this problem with this employee again. His warrior mentality came from **fear**.

Since those early days when I was overly aggressive and way too intimidating to be a good manager, I've learned that it is easier to make someone **want** to do something rather than **make** them do it. I try to mentor someone and encourage them to develop warrior mentality skills. A four-star general once gave me a good visual of this principal by laying a string on a table. He told me to pull it and I easily moved it across the table. Then he told me to push it. When I tried, it bunched up and was difficult to move in the direction I wanted.

He looked at me with a wry grin and told me that's how I should lead. Lead and you will pull folks along and they will follow you. Try to push them and they will balk and resist, making it much more difficult for you to get where you want to go. This proved to be a valuable lesson in teaching warrior mentality. *It is more helpful to show by your example than to preach it.*

Warrior mentality can also be learned by following those whom you observe achieving success first hand.

Recently I've been mentoring the young manager of my hunting plantation in the fine art of whitetail hunting. I've hunted these animals for decades and the amount of respect I have for them knows no bounds. A mature trophy buck is very intelligent, has huge ears that can detect even the slightest sound, a nose that can wind you a mile away, a sixth sense that seems to alert him to danger, and wonderful eyes that can detect the slightest movement along with eye properties that allow him to see in the dark which makes the buck mainly nocturnal. These animals are crafty and travel through impenetrable thickets, exposing themselves for only a few moments before disappearing like ghosts. Harvesting a mature trophy whitetail buck year after year is exceedingly difficult, and it takes patience, skill, perseverance, and a warrior mentality.

Matching wits with a mature whitetail buck is one of my favorite things to do in life. It is as exciting and rewarding as any endeavor that I've undertaken I find a huge buck and tirelessly hunt him all year and might see him once or twice. When one is finally harvested, it is truly a time of celebration.

I preach hunting lore such as this to this youngster constantly, but unfortunately most of it goes in one ear and out the other with little retention.

I am a person who is disciplined and dedicated far beyond the norm. I study the land, I look for trophy buck sign, I find where he feeds and beds down, and I plan strategy of how to position myself to have a chance of seeing him no matter what time of day. Then I assiduously hunt *every* morning, middle of the day, and evening. I generally lose weight during this time of year because of the tremendous effort that I expend.

My manager, on the other hand, likes to sleep in, especially if the weather is nasty and bitterly cold. I've taught him how to scout, read the signs, where to put up deer stands, and the habits of whitetail bucks and he is well versed and thoroughly trained on all of it, but he has not achieved the warrior mentality of giving it his all; consequently he has never bagged one.

He watched me pursue my trophy buck morning, noon, and night in fair and foul weather without fail, but after hunting days on end I had not even seen my big deer and I think he was amused by it to a degree. Then one evening everything worked out perfectly and I bagged him. He was a monster buck of a lifetime, and seeing this huge buck set my young manager on fire. The next morning he was on his deer stand an hour before daylight. All my cajoling, scolding, and encouraging fell on deaf ears, but when he got the call to come help me put that giant deer in the truck that afternoon it was the key that unlocked the cage that housed his warrior mentality and freed it. Seeing all my effort rewarded before his own eyes somehow made it all worthwhile to him and he vowed to relentlessly pursue his own big buck of a lifetime. LOL - Sadly his warrior mentality was short lasting and almost as quickly as he got fired up his flame went out and he went back to sleeping in. He only lasted maybe two days.

Ugh!

Okay, so what do you need to unlock your cage? Fear? Great leadership? Gentle mentoring? Seeing someone else succeed? Whatever it is, FIND IT! I don't care if you are building your business, trying to lose weight, climbing a mountain, learning to play the guitar, writing a book, closing a deal, or attempting to bag a trophy whitetail, success will not come without fighting for it like a raging warrior.

And remember above all else God is the One who can help you the most. Ask and you will receive. He wants you to win!

Don't you realize that in a race everyone runs,
but only one person gets the prize? So run to win!
−1 Cor, 9:24

CHAPTER 7

Warrior Mentality

Jamie Vrinios

The warrior mentality is not something we are born with it is *earned* when an individual has developed the qualities of perseverance, determination, courage, faith, and strength. *Warriors* are bold, fearless, and selfless individuals driven by a cause and inspired to RISE UP with RELENTLESS COURAGE through any challenge. They go into every battle with a single-minded, willful focus to WIN at all cost. Leaders with a warrior mentality are the ones you want by your side because they are willing to be on the *front* lines with you. They are by far the most fierce and loyal individuals you could ever encounter and passionate in defending what is right and defeating the wrongs.

If you are fortunate enough to encounter warriors you will be transformed from the beginning because they will call out the excuses in your life that prevent you from living out your purpose. These warriors have a *contagious spirit* and will inspire you to get up and fight for your dreams—quitting or giving up does not exist in their vocabulary. To develop a warrior mentality, you must be willing to have Level 10 Honest conversations with yourself and with these sage warriors as you declare war on every single excuse that has held you back in the past or that will try to invade your mind in the future. The warrior mentality summons you to operate with ZERO DOUBT, to NEVER GIVE UP and keep fighting until the battle is won. When you have made a commitment to WIN and have developed a warrior mentality there is no going back.

Picture the commander in chief of an army leading his troops into battle and the mentality demanded of him before he even begins. Could you ever imagine a general taking his soldiers into battle and after the first gunshot running away? The soldiers who trusted him with their lives on the battlefield would be left on the battlefield wondering what to do. It's no different with you and your dreams. There is no turning back when you have a warrior mentality. The obstacles that could take the average person out of the battle are only GO signals for the warrior to get up and FIGHT. If you stay IN the battle until the victory is won you will be consumed with the WIN, never the pain. Warriors are focused on the FINISH and never the FIGHT.

Now let's compare that to the individual who chooses to GIVE UP after the first fiery dart is sent their way. The one who quits will live with regret the rest of their life while the battle wounds of a warrior will soon heal and the victory will remain. The quitter mentality is so far removed from that of the warrior that it can be difficult for the two to coexist in many cases. The warrior has zero tolerance for the quitter, who is apathetic, self-focused, and far too lazy to think about helping those around him. The sluggard serves nobody but himself, and this mentality goes diametrically against the very core of a warrior.

"The soul of the sluggard craves and gets nothing,
while the soul of the diligent is richly supplied"
– (Proverbs 13:4).

You may wonder why the warrior is relentless in helping those who are suffering in the world and the dreamers who have a desire to WIN. I believe the answer is this: Every great warrior has overcome the darkest of days in their life, which yields the discernment to feel others pain. It is the pain that drives a warrior to help others cross over so they too can FINISH WELL. If you are praying for answers and God sends you a warrior, whatever you do, do NOT run away. It's the signal for you to RUN FASTER toward your DREAMS, to RISE UP and CONQUER your fears. Just remember when you get to the other side of your greatest battles it is your turn to PASS IT ON and encourage others to do the same.

The training ground for every warrior is different and may begin at various stages of life, so remember this, the GIANT that is in front of you is NEVER bigger than the God who lives IN YOU. My training ground began very early in my life. As a little girl, I had a quiet place in my closet, and looking back at it now it was my place of refuge, my "prayer" closet—my "war room." I would go there often because it felt like the safest space I could find in my house. The prayers that I prayed were not the normal prayers of a little girl; they were the prayers of a "warrior in training" because the house I was living in was a battleground every single day. It didn't matter how many times I would cry out to God for the violence to end, I was still forced to face one more day in an environment in which I never felt safe.

I remember the reading light I had tucked in the corner of the closet with various books, and among them was my Bible. I would read it daily and ask God to help me just one more day, and that is exactly what He did. I was never angry with God as a child, every time I went to pray I could feel His love all around me ministering to my spirit. My conversations with Him were not the most eloquent of prayers. In fact they were quite simple, and the main theme in every prayer was: God please help me, protect me, and remove me from this environment.

I know this prayer might sound crazy to some but to the individual who is in the middle of a battle you are only looking at what is directly in front of you and for me it meant survival for one more day. I learned early on that the battles are won DAILY. God eventually answered my prayers, and I know the abuse I observed and endured as a young child was never God's will but it was God who I learned to lean on to help me through my early warrior-in-training years. Today He continues to be the one who LEADS me through every battle in my life.

The thing you must know about God is HE is GOOD and He is your FRIEND. You may ask why I am sharing this with you and how this is a key to developing a warrior mentality. I believe with my entire being that when you know that God is WITH YOU this gives you the faith, strength, and courage to overcome every battle in life.

For God hath not given us the spirit of fear; but of power, and of love, and of a sound mind" – (2 Timothy 1:7).

Every obstacle in our life is another opportunity to look deep inside ourselves and summon the STRENGTH to endure what we never thought was possible. As I look back on my life, I know it is by the grace of God I have been able to conquer what many perceived to be insurmountable obstacles. An individual with a Level 10 warrior mentality has a clear understanding that they must GIVE IT ALL if they want to see the miraculous. Many pray for miracles and are relying on God to make things happen in their lives, but what you must realize is that God will never do for you what He has given you the ability to accomplish and overcome. Fortunately, that includes anything within His will for your life.

> *"Jesus looked at them and said, 'With man this is impossible, but with God all things are possible'"*
> – (Matthew 19:26).

Warrior mentality is developed by GIVING IT YOUR ALL! And just when you think you've given it your ALL and can't go another step, something inside enables you to persevere, and that is when the STRENGTH and FAITH you never knew you had RISE UP and give you the relentless courage to SOAR. Many will give up during this metamorphosis stage of a warrior, but to those who choose to RISE, they are the ones who will SOAR on the wings of brave eagles.

> *"But those who trust in the Lord will find new strength. They will soar high on wings like eagles. They will run and not grow weary. They will walk and not faint"*
> – (Isaiah 40:31).

The Molting Stage of the Eagle

An eagle will go through a "molting" process in their lifespan. This is a wilderness time that all eagles will face. Some eagles live for about 30 years, and at some point in their lives they begin to lose their feathers, beak, and talons. During this time, the eagle will walk, like a turkey does, because it lacks the strength to fly. At this time the eagle will choose some area of a mountain where the sun can shine directly on it. It will lie on a rock and bathe in the sun. The molting eagle understands what is happening and will scratch its talons down to the nubs and knock its beak off to rid it of the "calcium deposit build up," after it has pulled out all of its feathers. The eagle becomes completely vulnerable and many die at this point. During this time, some have observed eagles coming and dropping food to the ones going through this "molting" stage. Yet it is never the younger eagles that are dropping the food, it is always the older eagles that have survived this experience and know what the "molting" eagle is going through. After this miserable waiting period, which lasts for an interminable amount of time as its feathers, beak, and talons grow back, the eagle suddenly RISES UP and SOARS again with more beauty and greater strength than ever before!

In 2010 I had begun to believe the greatest battles of my life were behind me, but I was wrong. In fact, I would find myself in a fierce fight just to stay alive. I was staring at myself in the mirror and I could hardly recognize the 90-pound skeleton-like appearance of the woman looking back at me. Regardless of my devastating illness, I was the sole breadwinner for our family and had forced myself to continue to work. I vividly remember a trip I took to Chicago to speak when I was at my weakest point. I only made it through that exhausting, difficult trip because God gave me enough strength to speak just one more time;

CRAZY LIKE FOXES

otherwise I couldn't physically have done it.

I will never forget the event that occurred after speaking that night. I went back to my administrative assistant, Natalie Beckley's, home in Illinois. When I arrived, she took one look at me without my suit jacket on and I could see the look of FEAR on her face. She told me I HAD to find out what was wrong with me, and NOW. She knew if I didn't, my body would shut down and I would die. I'd been fighting through this ordeal for months and the doctors had no answers. When I first developed symptoms I thought it was no big deal, and I was confident that the antibiotics the doctors gave me would take care of my illness within a couple of weeks.

The first dosage of antibiotics would lead to many more variations as the doctors tried to find the right medicine to kill whatever it was that was depriving me of every single nutrient that I put in my body. The weeks led to months, and my body was shedding pounds daily. Every time I ate anything it would go right through me within an hour. I had absolutely no control over my bowels, and my body was so weak that it was difficult for me to work. I was so determined not to allow anything to stop me from my speaking engagements that I would fast and wear an adult diaper as I traveled. The attack on my body was violent and extremely unpredictable, so eating food on my trips was not something I did. I simply refused to eat while I traveled in fear of having an accident while on a plane or onstage.

I knew I needed prayer, but I only wanted those praying for me who truly believed I would be healed, and the few prayer warriors with whom I surrounded myself were only

BOB WILLIAMSON AND JAMIE VRINIOS

those who BELIEVED 100 percent in my healing.

A warrior wants to talk only to another warrior when going through battles. It is no different from the eagles helping eagles that have experienced a "molting period." I am so grateful that I had Pastor Andrew and Beth Piland pray with me and show me scriptures that would speak life to my "spirit." If they had not helped me walk through this battle I believe things might have turned out differently.

The warriors God places in your life encourage you to keep going, and just like the eagles, they will drop badly needed nourishment from on high, but it's up to us to FIGHT. Many people have asked me about this life shock and why I never shared it with the world while I was going through it. I don't share my pain with others unless they have a warrior mentality, and you shouldn't either if you want to conquer the molting periods in your life. I was focused on the FINISH and I knew I would share the VICTORY in due time.

I have always been the sole provider for my family and there was absolutely no way I could lie down and die, so I gave myself no other option but to get up and fight every single day. I would meditate daily for hours on the word of God and my focus stayed on the VICTORY. I spent day after day praying and walking on the beach as I collected an enormous number of sand dollars. Today when I look at the jars of them in my home they are a constant reminder of what it REALLY means to have FAITH.

A warrior mentality is built on FAITH, and everything else follows. In the beginning of my diagnosis, I felt strong and was up for the fight, but as the days turned into weeks, then months I was not sure if I could go one more day. I had never experienced any kind of serious illness prior to this and was always proud of the fact that my energy level was so high. I found out very quickly that our physical body can give up on us and it is the "spirit of a man or woman" that really matters when surviving becomes the objective. It was when I was crying out to God for Him to please take me to heaven or heal me that I finally found the answer I needed. I really did not feel I had the strength to continue, but after my daily prayers the peace of God would fill my heart and renew my strength one more day. I learned that spiritual food was what I needed to feed myself if I was going to LIVE! You see, on the outside my body was like the eagle with no feathers, weak, frail, and vulnerable, but my "inner man" was growing stronger because I was leaning on God and His power, not mine.

"That is why we never give up. Though our bodies are dying, our spirits are being renewed every day" – (2 Corinthians 4:16).

An individual with a warrior mentality understands this principle because they have walked through the "darkest of valleys" and came out BRAVER THAN EVER. The irony to this season of my life was that it brought me back to the days in my closet, the cold nights with no heat, the prayers that were answered, and that I came out of it on the other side. Think about that when you feel like you are not sure you can go another day. Reflect on the victories you've had in your life when you go through hard times. You will be encouraged!

Memories were flooding my mind of the holidays when

I was alone and suicidal, and yet somehow, I made it! The reason I could RISE UP and SOAR is because I was reminded of my victories in life and that God was with me then and He is with me now. Level 10 warriors understand the power in their prayer closet, the weakest moments when we are facedown on the ground is when God's power is the greatest. His strength is perfect when our strength is gone. Each time He said,

"My grace is all you need. My power works best in weakness. So now I am glad to boast about my weaknesses, so the power of Christ can work through me" – (2 Corinthians 12:9).

After many months of the violent attack on my body I was determined to get up ONE MORE TIME. I got up from my knees that day and made the decision to take another long walk on the beach. When I arrived, the clouds were dark and it was about to storm, but I saw a rainbow in the middle of the clouds. When I saw the rainbow my spirit leapt and I smiled big. I knew God was reminding me of His promises.

For an individual who has lived life without falling to their knees and crying out to God for answers this might be difficult to relate to, but when you have arisen from your molting period and transformed into a Level 10 warrior mentality you will understand. The inner strength of a warrior is what gives you the ability to pursue God's purpose in your life unapologetically. As I was walking down that deserted beach I saw a man standing in the water by himself. He was an older man, and I couldn't believe he was in the water with all the lightning there'd been. Nobody else was in sight on the beach, and the words he spoke to me were very clear. He asked, "How far do you have to go?" I replied, "Not very far." He answered back, "Well when the rain comes, it comes fast." I smiled as I replied to him (and myself), "Yes, it does."

I just knew at that moment that God had sent me a messenger to remind me that my prayers were answered. The rain started pouring and I just kept walking and thanking God for answering my prayers. The symptoms were still there but it didn't matter. I knew He answered my prayers and it was just a matter of time before I would see it manifest in the natural. The vision you have right now for your life is no different. It's just a matter of time before your dreams will come true if you will develop a warrior mentality and believe it before you see it in the natural.

"Faith is the confidence that what we hope for will actually happen. It gives us assurance about things we cannot see" – (Hebrews 11:1).

Soon after my walk that day I was introduced to the integrative doctors who would properly diagnose me with having parasites that I ingested when I was speaking in the Ukraine. They assisted me in the complete healing of my body. The healing crisis took months and I got a lot worse before I was completely healed, but I kept moving toward my destiny anyway. How did I navigate through this and keep going? I stayed focused on the FINISH not the FIGHT and GAVE IT MY ALL!

The eagle that fights through its molting season so it can SOAR to NEW HEIGHTS discovers that it has a greater strength than ever before. We are no different in this transformational process to a brave beginning in our life. Nobody can take the journey for you and even though there are more experienced warriors that may give you food through the process, ultimately YOU must choose to GIVE IT ALL YOU HAVE if you want to reach your full potential in life. There was not one person who could believe for me, I had to find that strength within myself and you must do the same.

"What defines us is how well we rise after falling."
– Unknown

So take a minute and rate yourself right now on a scale of 1 to 10, with 1 being a total wimp and 10 a warrior in response to pressure. How well do you rise after you fall? Do you give up easily? If you want to develop a warrior mentality decide now to never give up!

The choice that you make to arise or give up will impact your life and those connected to you. What message does your life speak to those around you? Is it inspiring? Would you agree that we instinctively know when someone has a Level 10 warrior mentality? You just can't deny it—it is the warrior you always call on when you need good advice or trouble knocks on your door.

A mother's love for her child is something that nobody can possibly understand except our Heavenly Father. It is impossible for me to understand a mother who could hurt or abandon a child, and that includes my own mother disowning my children and me 31 years ago. I would dare to say that the loss of a child is a mother's greatest pain, and the fear of losing a child or seeing them in distress will put a mother on her knees. The love I have for my children is FIERCE, and that has been evident by the warrior mentality I have demonstrated throughout their lives; however, nothing could have prepared me for the phone call I received from my son Nathan. The molting process I'd endured was the training ground for me to summon the relentless courage to overcome the GIANT in front of me. It is one thing to go through the battle when it concerns only you, but a different thing when the victory must be won to save the life of another.

It was about 1:30 p.m. on a sunny day in Florida. I was out on my lanai enjoying the weather when the phone rang. It was my son Nathan. I was expecting the enthusiastic sound of his voice to come through, but that day my son was in great danger and I only heard fear. He said, "Mom, I am in Jamaica and they are taking me to jail. There was a single bullet in my bag when I went through customs." Nathan was crying and told me he knew I was the only one he could count on and to please come fast. What he faced is a criminal offense and the sentence is five years or more in a foreign prison. He said, "Please take care of Virginia if I don't make it out of here." He was saying over and over how much he loved me. He told me there were police standing beside him while he made his call and they were taking him to jail immediately. The trial would be in the morning. I asked to speak to the police and I begged them to please let him go. I told them that he was a good man, but it was obvious they had another agenda. I knew it was not Nathan's bullet and I could sense over the phone that they had motives behind their decision that were not good. I got back on the phone and told him I loved him and that it was going to be okay, and he said, "Mom, I am so scared." I assured him he was not going to prison. I promised!

I kept it all together when I was on the phone with Nathan but as soon as I hung up, I screamed as loud as I could. I was crying out to God and begging Him to please protect my son and deliver him out of that prison. I went outside of my lanai and vomited several times because it felt like every demon in hell had punched the LIFE out of me. Once I threw up, I pulled it together and I made the decision to RISE UP! My choice was either RISE or curl up in a fetal position and give up. I owned a Level 10 warrior mentality by now and there was no way this battle was going to be lost!

If I had to rip off the prison doors myself, NOBODY was going to hurt my son. Every lesson I had learned in my life came together all at once with this ONE PHONE CALL. I had fought for my children their entire lives, but this battle was by far the FIERCEST and demanded that I would demonstrate relentless courage, strength, and faith like nothing I had ever experienced.

Nathan was released from that foreign prison but it was not without a FIGHT! He arrived home just 72 hours after that first phone call, and I was sitting in my driveway waiting for him to pull in. Nathan stepped out of the car and, as tears fell from my eyes, I hugged him tighter and longer than I had ever held anyone in my entire life. The thought of losing my son was by far the most frightening experience ever. If I hadn't developed a Level 10 warrior mentality the story would have ended very differently, and

I am absolutely positive of that!

It is amazing what we discover when we are willing to keep moving boldly with a fierce love and unwavering faith that strengthens not just our wings but the wings of those around us who have dialed our number and are praying we answer the call.

I am always moved to my core when I read the story of the Good Samaritan. This man was willing to answer the call. Can you imagine seeing a man beaten half to death on the side of the road and you just "walk on by"? The first guy was a priest who went to the other side of the road and just "passed by." The temple assistant saw a poor, beaten man and he chose to ignore him. It was the despised Samaritan who saved this man's life. Only he had the compassion to help a man in need. I bet the Good Samaritan recalled his "molting season," which made it impossible for him to just "walk on by."

When we read this story, it is shocking to think that anyone could just "walk on by" a hurting person, pretending they don't exist or thinking someone else will answer the call. Sadly, the truth is that there are people we pass by daily who are in deep pain, but many people will choose to just "walk on by." It is impossible for you to just "walk on by" when you have a warrior mentality.

How many people could be impacted by your decision right now to pursue your greatest potential and GIVE IT ALL YOU'VE GOT? If you want to WIN you must be bold!

"But the righteous are as bold as a lion" – (Proverbs 28:1).

When you walk in God confidence it bothers those who

believe in the safety zone of lukewarm. That's okay, because you will be ready for the "call." How many times have you held back and found out later your God-given boldness could have shifted a life, or maybe even a nation.

Where are the men and women with a warrior mentality? A lukewarm mind-set has never inspired a soul because it requires no faith. But the individual who has a "fire" inside his soul is absolutely UNSHAKEABLE.

"I survived because the fire inside of me burned brighter than the fire around me." – Unknown

If you want to WIN you must have the fire inside! If you want to WIN you must have faith! If you want to WIN you must be braver than ever! If you want to WIN you must be courageous! If you want to SOAR, you must rise up and develop the "wings of a warrior."

EPILOGUE

Writing this book was quite the adventure. We both are certified type A, high D personalities. We have independently achieved a lofty degree of success and thus think we are right concerning just about everything. We have strong personalities, are stubborn, opinionated, sometimes overbearing, and have quite different writing styles. And after spending many months working together on this book it required significant effort on both of our parts to avoid exacting bodily harm on each other and remain friends.

Seriously, we discovered that though we differ in so many ways including age, gender, personality, and life experiences, we have strikingly similar beliefs on what it takes to succeed.

We consider this book to be the foundation for beginning your journey to achieve great things. If you have learned nothing else, we hope by now that you understand that you can succeed far beyond your wildest dreams, providing you are determined to work hard and smart and not ever consider quitting.

It is not lost on us that we could not share everything that will help you achieve your dreams in this one book. Our primary desire and motivation is to help those of you who are willing to give it your best to break through mediocrity and go on to wildly succeed. In that light, we are contemplating expanding Crazy Like Foxes to include other books that we feel will prove essential in that regard.

Additionally, we are working toward supplementing the books with quarterly workbook/day planners that will provide daily encouragement and should help you organize and manage your time efficiently. Live coaching is another tool under discussion that we believe will benefit you enormously.

Basically, we are determined to share the lifetimes of experience and know-how of two highly successful/high-net-worth people to detail exactly how we did it. It is a way for us to give back, and we are driven to do that. We both believe that our Lord and Savior desires that we help others. Some might call that "crazy," and we say, "Sure it is, Crazy Like Foxes."